PATSY CLAIRMONT

W Publishing Group

An Imprint of Thomas Nelson

Published in Nashville, Tennessee, by W Publishing Group. W Publishing is a registered trademark of Thomas Nelson, Inc.

Thomas Nelson, Inc., titles may be purchased in bulk for educational, business, fund-raising, or sales promotional use. For information, please e-mail SpecialMarkets@ThomasNelson.com.

Patsy Clairmont is represented by Mike Atkins Entertainment, Inc.

The websites recommended in this book are intended as resources for the reader. These websites are not intended in any way to be or to imply an endorsement on behalf of Thomas Nelson, nor does the publisher vouch for online content for the life of this book.

Unless otherwise cited, Scripture quotations are taken from THE NEW KING JAMES VERSION. © 1982 by Thomas Nelson, Inc. Used by permission. All rights reserved.

Scripture quotations marked KJV are taken from the KING JAMES VERSION of the Bible. Public domain.

Scripture quotations marked NIV are taken from the HOLY BIBLE, NEW INTERNATIONAL VERSION®. © 1973, 1978, 1984, 2011 by Biblica Inc.™ Used by permission. All rights reserved worldwide. www.zondervan.com.

Italics added to Scripture quotations are the author's own emphasis.

Library of Congress Control Number: 2013940556

ISBN-13 9780849947636

Printed in the United States of America

13 14 15 16 17 RRD 6 5 4 3 2

To the "Franklin Campus," who are visionary twirlers: thank you for inspiring me.

contents

introduction

I love a good twirl.

Okay, I confess: it's been awhile since I have spun in circles like a pinwheel. When I was a kid, after twirling in circles, I would topple to the ground in a heap of giggles and wait for the world to stop tumbling. I felt like I was inside a kaleidoscope on spin cycle. Once my head cleared I'd jump back up and do it again.

Today I can simply stand up too quickly and I feel tipsy! Somehow, that's not as much fun. In fact, I take pills for it. But when I think back to my childhood, I thought dizziness was worth a good spin.

If your life is as busy as mine, and I believe it is, then you probably feel like you're in a whirl as you gyrate from one activity to another. And if you are like me, you can get so dizzy that you forget what's important. It's the old tyranny of the urgent. We do what we think we have to, and sometimes in the doing we can ignore what truly matters. I know I can.

I love the word *twirl*. It's an energy word, one with revolutions that allow us, in a breathtaking swirl, to enter our lives with purpose and joy. But *twirl* can also be a word that leaves us exhausted and depleted. So you will notice the word being used to pick us up, which is this book's intention, and to caution us of the dizziness that takes us down. Like life, which can be good or bad, *twirl* can be high or low.

That's not to say there aren't seasons where breakneck speed isn't necessary. I recognize hurry-up is part of the human dilemma. But when frenzy becomes a lifestyle and harried becomes our uniform, it's time to put on the brakes and reevaluate. Because right after harried comes bitter, sad, and depressed. I have careened around on the back roads of depression, peered over its dangerous ledges, and even parked in its dark caves. I don't recommend the views.

Twirl (this book) is meant to help realign our spin on life so we can proceed with intentionality, remembering in the midst of hardship and responsibility to choose activities that lead to renewal. Our God is a Redeemer and Restorer. And I love that he invites us to be an active participant in this life with Christ's leadership, and to learn how to take care of ourselves while contributing to others' lives in ways that won't rupture our heart or invade their privacy.

I would love for us to choose a saner path than the one swirling with splintering options. Exhaustion has become society's badge of honor—and those who succumb, a driven people. Jesus calls us to be a peculiar people who frequent peace-filled resting places and high towers of refuge. He offers to guide us along a narrow road full of dignity, purpose, gratitude, and rest.

While we are given the opportunity to make healthy choices, we can sometimes feel divided by the pull of too many options and too many voices calling our name. *Twirl* reminds us of things that matter. These chapters are like Post-It notes for our heart. Some may fit you and some may not, so lean into the ones that do.

I've been around the block of life so many times, I've worn out the curbs. Along the way I've learned, often the hard way, what cheers a heart and what cheats a heart. It is my desire to be a cheerleader in the highest sense. Perhaps, through my experience, I can save you a few hard knocks, and together we can celebrate what matters.

The chapters may seem eclectic, and they are, which tends to be my style anyway; but the book is tied together by the ribbons of "what matters." What matters in our lives when all is said and all is sung. I have a sign in my bookcase as a reminder:

Enjoy the little things in life, for
one day you will realize they were
the big things.—Robert Brault

The topics in this offering go from dance to depression, from daffodils to death, from tree planting to picture taking . . . maybe I should have had a merry-go-round on the cover instead of a pinwheel. But the pinwheel's breath-driven spin puts me in mind of a life filled with the breath of God, turning in such a way that it brings joy and then flutters to a stop. Life can come at us in spasms of extremes, couched in busy, so I just wanted to say to myself and my friends: let's step off the merry-go-round and slow down long enough not to miss what matters.

Understand that going from nine-aught-nothing to absolute stillness can be startling and awkward at best. Those of us who find our value in full-speed-ahead might initially wonder if we are wasting our time, when instead of being activity-bound we are slowing down to meditate, garden, and soak in bubbles up to our earlobes. Trust me, the benefits of our gawky efforts will be worth the peace-giving results. Besides, this isn't a book about stopping, necessarily, but about regaining perspective and not missing out on things that anchor our soul.

There's something about a sane person who has a pulse on her life, one who is setting healthy limits, who is winsome, enviable, and honorable. So if you need to shift gears to achieve that kind of existence, you may need to give yourself permission to feel different in the process, because *new* is an adjustment. Whether it's a new attitude, new song, new perspective, new centeredness, or a new settledness.

A few years ago an out-of-town friend paid a visit, and after a couple of days she said to me, "There's something different about you. I've been trying to figure it out. It's like your insides are quieter."

Honestly, that was one of the best compliments I'd ever had. I had been through a corridor of what felt like, at the time, exhaust-ing changes. I knew God had done a fresh work in me to tame my frenzy, but it was sweet to have a friend who knew me well recog-nize it too.

We forget that others "feel" our insides when we have exchanges with them, which is why they say things to us like, "Are you okay? You seem _____" (fill in the blank: preoccupied, angry, sad, etc.). When we step over the line of multitasking to shredding our energies, others can feel our inner exhaustion and they sense the distraction and depletion that comes with weariness.

So join me as we shift into a lower gear with a fresh perspective.

The design of this tome allows busy people to enter in wherever you like. Front, back, or middle, enjoy a chapter or half a dozen— you can make it fit into a short session of reading or an evening of reflections. Perhaps sitting with the questions at the end of the chapters will be helpful.

Come, and together we will number the stars, dance with daffodils, sidle up to joy, test our wings, hold a song close to our heart, bundle letters, and do many other worthwhile exercises. All with the intentions of securing our sanity, adding to our vitality, and fulfilling our destiny.

How I love that we can't be too young or too old, too broken or bruised, too tired or tattered for God to work in us! His mercies are new every morning. That means as long as we live we have access to the storehouses of God, so bring your shopping cart and let's twirl down the aisles of his mercy and grace.

ONE

more

> *If the doors of perception were cleansed, everything would appear to man as it is—infinite.*
>
> —WILLIAM BLAKE

Did you know you are more than you realize? Inside of you are untapped veins of surprising potential.

It's true.

Not only that, but your friends, husband, boss, children—they are more as well. They have unexplored talent, hidden even from themselves. It's not the fact they have potential that surprises us, but it's the unexpected ways it comes out.

And then there's God's limitlessness. Talk about "more." We think at times we have the Lord figured out so we can fully explain him to others, when—*kaboom!*—he explodes our theories. God is not bound by time or even our theology. He can't be conveniently contained or tidied up to fit our beliefs. He is so much more.

This is great news.

For one thing, when we understand our potential to be more than we know, it allows us to break free from other people's opinions. In fact, when my sister-in-law Candy was a child, she would cry if you said the word *opinion*. We think it was the word *pin* that made it sound threatening to her. And actually it can be painful to have people's narrow judgments pin us down. Especially if we buy into their assessment and allow it to restrict our development.

I watched a child who was continually told she was clumsy grow up, and it became a self-fulfilling prophecy. To this day she trips over gnats and is bound by the duct tape of people's criticism. But in the same way I've also seen youngsters grow into more than I thought possible because they had people around them with open-handed grace. Somehow grace adds space for people's uncharted hearts to be safely explored.

I have to remind myself that people can restrict us only with our permission. As children we are vulnerable, but once we grow into our adult years we are instructed to "put away childish things" (1 Corinthians 13:11). It seems to me that one of those childish things is the judgment of others that comes from their brokenness and ignorance. Unfortunately I have been on both sides of that human ailment. I have been the one being critical and the one who had criticism heaped on her. Giving up my childish right to hold a grudge toward the "heapers" in my life has accelerated my healing and deepened my realization and compassion for my own inconsistencies.

We are fragile people . . . yet full of surprises.

About a dozen years ago we were visiting with friends when my husband, Les, was asked if he could go back in time what he would choose to do as an occupation. Well, we'd been married almost forty years at that time, so I knew with certainty what his answer would be. Actually, I knew a list of jobs he would have valiantly pursued. But when he said something that was not on the list, I was confused. I mean, it made perfect sense when I thought about it, but how in forty years had it never come up?

I'm telling you, there's more to folks than we realize. Just about the time we think there's nothing they could do that would surprise us . . . they do. They are like piñatas, chock-full of unexpected goodies.

Years ago, when I slowly emerged from my agoraphobic restrictions, I began learning things about myself I didn't know, nor did others. I remember a friend commenting after seeing my new spin on our living room arrangement that she didn't know I could decorate. After she left I thought about her comment. I realized I'd never given her reason to know because I couldn't handle people's judgment if I didn't do it "right." So I didn't risk it at all. When I began letting go of doing things perfectly, I gradually began to venture into untested territory. Guess what I found out? I love decorating . . . in my own bohemian way. It's an artsy expression that pleases me because it helps tie me into the creative heart of God.

Risk is risky. Yes, you may quote me. Risk means we don't

know the outcome; it could go in our favor or work against us. The "against us" part was the threat that held me back. For years I didn't have the internal flexibility to withstand rejection and what felt like condemnation, which I was already heaping on myself.

I allowed a great deal of my worth to hang on other people's opinions. And I often treated their opinions as my gospel, in that I allowed their assessments to govern my life. No wonder the scripture on renewing the mind became so important to my recovery. I needed a new understanding of the gospel, one that offered me liberty.

> And do not be conformed to this world,
> but be transformed by the renewing
> of your mind, that you may prove
> what *is* that good and acceptable and
> perfect will of God. (Romans 12:2)

It wasn't that I didn't know the Liberator; it was I didn't know how to exchange my shaky beliefs for the truth of who I was in Christ. That's where I'd find my freedom, in his forgiveness and his promise of a future and a hope. I began studying Scripture, meditating, and praying . . . and ever so slowly, the seeded lies were dislodged from my beliefs. I joined a Bible study group in my community and developed friendships with women who were secure enough in their identities to affirm me, and ones who modeled social graces that I lacked. That was restorative. I became more aware of God's daily kindnesses toward me.

The Lord knows we are more because he designed us. Rest on that thought for a moment. God thought us up. Isn't that amazing?

He created us for a purpose, and as long as there is breath in our bodies we can grow, change, and become more, much more than we expected.

My friend Karen joined our poetry class, not realizing how many beautiful words nested inside of her. I watched her take on the class challenges with a full heart of vulnerability, which caused her unspoken words to spill out into poetic word pictures. Every week Karen would shake her head in wonder and say, "I don't know where this is coming from. I didn't know it was in me." It's been lovely to watch the poet in her bloom and to witness her half-formed thoughts find shape and expression.

We are more than we know.

Recently friends came for a visit. I had not seen my friend's husband in close to forty years. He knew me when I was still working through the sticky wickets of agoraphobia leftovers. I wasn't housebound by then, but I was living a restricted life based on my anxiety. At one point in our conversation he said, "Did you ever expect you'd be traveling, speaking, and writing?"

"No," I confessed.

"Me either," he admitted. "I told my friends who have heard you speak, that is not the Patsy I knew."

"I'm as surprised as you are," I said, wagging my head.

I had no idea what God's plan was for me. Had I known I'm sure I would have pulled a Jonah and hotfooted it down to Joppa. I would not have believed I could have traveled this cross-country, public path I've been on for the past thirty-eight years. Remember me, the agoraphobic? What was God thinking, saying, *Lights, cameras, action?*

We are more than we know.

Last year, like my friend Karen, I, too, joined my first poetry class. My bones were bruised from knocking because even though I had written an armload of books, I had not explored the inner landscape of poetry. I, too, was surprised by the words that poured out of me. First a trickle, then a stream, and at times a river. I think what surprised me most was how revealing my poems were about my heart. It became therapy. One of our assignments was about feet, and since I've traveled for so many years, this is what came out:

Feet of a Million Miles

Traversing craggy hills of hardship,
Stinging sands of unspoken sympathies,
Valleys of deep regret . . .
March on

Just ahead: rivers,
Rainbows,
And silver-flecked sunsets,
Amber with hope.

Step lively your treck nears a turn,
Where flowers weep tomorrow's seeds,
And sparrows rise to ride rain clouds.
You'll rest soon.

I have had fun sharing my poetry with friends. Some like it; others not so much. It has been interesting to find that I'm not swayed by either response, pro or con, because I finally, finally . . . recognize that I am a work in progress. Sometimes growth can only be measured by where we've been, not by what others are doing. (You might want to back up and read that sentence again.)

There's more to me than I know. Golly, it's taken me a whole lifetime to figure that out.

Don't take that long. Start now. Believe for more. Believing helps bring into the light that which has been tucked inside you all along.

Remember there's a difference between an opinion of man and a principle of God. Our more-ness is a direct result of his much-ness. It's not about our ability, but his generosity. It's about the Giver of light and every good gift.

Embrace it . . . you are more than you know.

1. This week, try a conversation with someone you know that offers them space to discover some of their more. Ask questions to help spur them to search inside, but be careful not to violate their privacy.

2. Name three things you'd like to do in your lifetime that you haven't already done.

3. If you had a jet to fly anywhere in the world, where would you go? What five people would you take with you?

4. If you could play an instrument for your personal enjoyment, what would it be?

5. What color would you choose to represent your life?

TWO

yes

I thank you God for this most amazing day, for the leaping
greenly spirits of trees, and for the blue dream of sky and for
everything which is natural, which is infinite, which is yes.

—E. E. CUMMINGS

Don't you love the word *yes*? It's so joyful and cooperative,
and it's such a door opener. Just saying *yes* can make us and others
smile. Try it. Say it out loud. See. You smiled, didn't you? Yes has its
roots in happy. And who doesn't need more of both?

Yes can be a skylight for the soul, it can aerate our attitudes, and it can be a bridge over misunderstandings. *Yes* is a seal of approval, an Enter Here sign, a "permission granted" document. *Yes* is powerful, permissive, and pleasing . . . most of the time.

Imagine the length of this *yes*. Karam and Kartari Chand were married for eighty-eight years and thirty-three days. Wow. As I write this, that's one of the longest recorded marriages. I wonder, after the first seventy years did he still remember to take out the garbage and did she still gripe about his manners?

One of my biggest *yeses* was on my wedding day fifty-one years ago July. That's right, fifty-one years. My husband, Les, and I are amazed that we have survived each other, since we both are a bit much. We are taken aback that the years have flown by. Karam and Katari's record both encourages us and scares us.

Only yesterday we were kids holding hands while walking the Lake Superior shoreline in Michigan, and the next thing we knew we were in rocking chairs side by side on our Tennessee porch waiting for our Social Security checks. Years turned into photo albums and senior discounts. Somehow, even though aging is the natural progression of life, when we said yes, we didn't actually expect to get old like our parents. Yet here we are, smack-dab in the middle of prescriptions, indigestion, and leg cramps.

Today when Les and I wake up, we aren't as flexible as we once were, so our leap out of bed is more like a rolling groan; but we sure are grateful to still be here. It just sounds different than our youthful squeals of delight at the dawn of a new day. We continue to learn, though, that a *yes* to God helps us enter even our limitations with more gusto.

No one grows old by living. Only by losing
interest in living.—Marie Beynon Ray

Trying to decide how to celebrate our fiftieth anniversary last year was a long discussion because Les and I had different views. There was no *yes* between us. I was thinking Paris; he was thinking we should rent a theater down the street from our house and show a movie. Movie? What? *A Series of Unfortunate Events?* C'mon, fifty years deserves France or Italy, not Bugs Bunny meets Daisy Duck at a tractor pull. But neither of us could find a yes for the other's ideas until . . . drum roll, please . . . we settled on an open house. Yep, open house. Sounds uh, well, dull, but I assure you it was a gala event.

It was an evening full of flowers, food, and magical music. Our front yard and porch, thanks to the effort of friends, looked like a swanky Paris café. Peonies filled the atmosphere inside and out like a summer festival. And the food . . . think food fair on steroids. It was a luscious array of goodies you'd expect at the queen's tea. And the music was, well, heavenly. A musician played an instrument called a Chapman Stick. If you haven't heard one, you should. It's as if a violin, guitar, and piano blended their voices to fill a room with a warm and glorious sound.

Oh, did I mention it was 104 degrees the day of our party? Well, it was. I noted that fact when the large frosting-flower slid off the wedding cake and splatted on the buffet. To cool down our guests so they, too, didn't splat, we strategically positioned fruited ice water, sweet tea, raspberry lemonade, and sodas on the front porch. Comedians Anita Renfroe and Ken Davis refreshed us with their style of entertainment. Anita's revision of our wedding vows left us in need of oxygen, as tears of laughter poured down our faces and splashed on our ankles. Over a hundred moist guests filed through the front door to wish us well. What a celebration! We shall carry it in our memories always . . . we hope. Les and I are so glad we both found a *yes* inside of ourselves for the gala event . . . and especially *yes* to each other on our wedding day.

Another huge *yes* in my life was when my heart opened to having God's truth as my guiding counsel. For years I was stuck in an emotional whirlpool, and it wasn't until I was being sucked under by a wave of desperation that my cry for help changed. Instead of expecting God to fix me, I told him I would do whatever he asked of me. From that time forward my life changed as I stopped talking about what I believed and began living it. It was as if *yes* unlocked a door within me. And I began a purposed study of God's Word and how to walk in it.

The first thing that I did was get out of bed, get dressed, and start functioning in my home. I began putting others' needs ahead of my fears, which were multiple, and I created new tapes for my mind. By that I mean my thought life was a tangle of negativity and criticism, so I began to memorize God's Word to repair misconceptions and maligning attitudes. I was awash in darkened thought cycles, so I chose verses that brought them into the light of truth.

For instance, I had a wretched view of my worth, so I began bathing my mind in Psalm 139. It was hard to believe that God was present when I was being knit together in my mother's womb, that I pleased him, and that he loved me. I began rehearsing these truths, especially when I was in another tirade at myself and making scathing judgments like, "You are so stupid," "You are so ugly,"

"You can't do anything right," "Nobody likes you." It takes effort to change destructive habits, so don't be disheartened when you slip back into an old pattern. Extend grace and mercy to yourself . . . God does. Then begin again choosing life.

My mental health recovery started with a *yes* to God and to myself. The Lord invites us to be a part of our recovery. So don't sit and wait for God to fix you; instead, get up and say yes to the Lord, to the new day, and to yourself.

Does that sound too simple? Too Pollyanna? Too *rah, rah, shish koom bah*? Trust me, I know how hard it is to change a lifestyle, a mind-set, and a belief system, because I have been in process for almost fifty years. I've never worked harder, and I'm still not done. No one is. None of us outgrows our need for assistance. I understand the toil and time involved in the tempering of a heart and the transforming of a mind, and I can say with a resounding *yes!* that it's worth the effort. Saying yes to Jesus was the path that led me to personal dignity, integrity, and to believing I had a God-given destiny.

By the way, set attainable goals so you don't position yourself to fail. Don't sabotage your own progress. Be sure to congratulate yourself for even small steps in the right direction. Be a cheerleader for yourself and others. This will take practice.

Yes is a radical word, whether it's a wedding *yes* or a Jesus *yes*. So be rad and go *yes* your world!

1. What has been your biggest *yes* to date?
2. What are three things you can do to improve your interior dialogue?
3. Have you said yes to Jesus as Lord? If not, how about today?

THREE

bloom

I wandered lonely as a cloud
That floats on high o'er vales and hills,
When all at once I saw a crowd,
A host, of golden daffodils;
Beside the lake, beneath the trees,
Fluttering and dancing in the breeze.

—WILLIAM WORDSWORTH

Hooray! The daffodils are in bloom! They shout, "Spring!"

I find the buttery petals visually invigorating. I'm influenced,

I'm sure, by the fact daffodils are the forerunners of many other delightful blooms to come. But there's just something about a burst of yellow after a dusky winter that cheers a heart and quickens one's pace. Our neighbors have several dozen daffodils in blossom as I write, and it makes me want to stop at their yard and join the dance.

Speaking of blooms you must see, Harold Harvey, a British painter, has an oil painting called *Picking Daffodils,* portraying a mother and daughter gathering daffodils in a field. It's so sweet and full of innocence. Just Google his name.

The impressionistic artist Claude Monet said:

> I must have flowers, always and
> always.—Claude Monet

I see why painters like Harvey, Monet, and Van Gogh headed with brush in hand for a vase or field full of flowers. Most of us are smitten by floral beauty, all the way from gaudy sunflowers touting their glory down to shy violets peeking out from under their green umbrellas.

How long has it been since you added blooms at your bedside, entryway, window ledge, and dressing table? It's a kind thing to do for yourself. Flowers are such an emotional boost. Almost as helpful as hormones (almost). And talk about a thoughtful gift to give a friend. We can, in one bouquet, give color, beauty, and fragrance—and we don't even have to wrap them!

Flowers are aligned with romance, love, motherhood, sympathy, ceremonies, holidays, and celebrations of all kind. From birthdays to communions to graduations and weddings you'll find blooms. If it's worth rejoicing over or weeping over, it's worth a floral statement.

I carried an orchid on a small white Bible on my wedding day fifty-one years ago. I still have the small Bible, and the memory of my orchid blooms on. For our fiftieth wedding anniversary we had a house full of flowers, which made our surroundings very festive and my heart so happy.

God could have chosen to begin life for mankind on a mountaintop, island, beach, or forest, but he chose a garden. Think about it. That's significant. God's signature is all over creation, but I think especially in our "little Edens." Our gardens are filled with a sense of his creative presence. God has amended the soil with life lessons, and the produce (flowers, fruits, vegetables) is meant to nurture us with truth and beauty and cause us to see him in all things.

Take, for instance, the seed. What a miracle! Get this: it has no brain, yet it knows exactly what it wants to be when it grows up. (Most of us are still trying to figure that out.) We never see zinnias strain to produce tomatoes, nor have I caught my petunias trying to be svelte lilies. Instead, this diminutive encasement follows its Creator's plan and purpose right up to the blossoms.

Have you ever considered that the seed is like a blueprint in that it contains all the information to produce not only a stem but also leaves, stamen, sepals, pistils, and blossoms? How did that much potential ever get stuffed inside something so tiny?

And another thing about this amazing nugget is that it's willing to do all its work out of the limelight, underground, and to allow the blooms to receive the applause. We never hear anyone say, "Wow, that was one great effort by that seed to produce such beauty. Hooray, seed!" Instead, we hear, "Oh, look at that flower. Isn't it spectacular?"

Yes, the garden flourishes with parables, from the seed that dies to give life, the single stem that pushes its way through concrete, to the tree that is damaged in the storm and grows more beautiful after the trauma.

Through the years I have had all size gardens. From a few lonely Johnny-jump-ups by my steps, to a side wildflower garden crowded with butterfly bushes, nasturtiums, and sweet Williams, to a back-yard subdivided into paths leading to five different growing areas. Today my "garden" is a few hanging baskets on my front porch and a fern on my back porch. Because life sometimes gets away from me, too, every year for the past four years I've promised myself a cluster of herbs on my side yard next to my kitchen. So I'm making sure this year I'll have parsley, sage, rosemary, and thyme. Or at least one fat tomato.

There's something so nurturing about watching a plant grow and then flourish. It's inspiring. I hope even if it's just a pot full of geraniums, with some ivy and candytuft, that you will nurture a little Eden in your corner of the world.

I must tell you about my green-thumb escapade with tulips. One year, when I lived in Michigan, I ordered scads of huge tulip bulbs to plant throughout our yard. Of course, we planted in the fall and then had to wait through a snowy winter before we'd see these spring beauties. That year we decided to take a winter break in the desert of California. When it was time to return to Michigan, one of my highlights was going to be seeing my "crop" of tulips in reds, yellows, and purples clustered on our property. But when we arrived home I saw only a smattering of blossoms, so I assumed the others had not yet come forth.

One day I was walking around in my yard surveying winter damage when a neighbor called to me. "Hey, Patsy, thank you." She waved.

Confused, I responded, "What for?" I waved back.

She ambled over to the fence and said, "For the tulips." She smiled.

Now I was befuddled. "What do you mean?" I didn't smile.

Well, here's the story she relayed. Seems after we left town, marauding squirrels dug up our lovely bulbs and replanted them throughout the neighborhood, like Robin Hood and his band. So when spring declared herself, our tulips lit up everyone's yards. I hadn't intended to share, but it certainly made her and the neighborhood happy.

If I were a flower I'd like to be a sunflower so I could have a view of all the other blossoms. Or a pansy because they always seem to be having so much fun with their friends. Or a morning glory twirling up a picket fence to hold my face to the full sun.

Truth is, I'm not a pansy, but I've been planted to be a Patsy. I began in a seed designed for a distinct purpose; to grow where I am planted and to bloom for as long as he gives me years.

In God's intentional bouquet which flower were you designed to be? A romantic rose? A playful daisy? An elegant iris?

And God said, "It is good."

Bloom, girlfriend, bloom.

God saw all that he had made, and it
was very good.—Genesis 1:31 NIV

1. What do you enjoy about a garden?

2. What flowers do you love to receive?

3. Have you ever, like Wordsworth, "wandered lonely as a cloud"? What cheered you?

FOUR
decorate

With the new day comes new strength and new thoughts.

—ELEANOR ROOSEVELT

I love to decorate and redecorate my house. For instance, I'm forever changing the landscape of our living room, which can drive my hubby banana-crackers. Les doesn't understand my need to pull, push, tug, and drag pieces of furniture from hither to yon (and back again), but after fifty-one years of living with me, he tolerates my urges.

I tend to do the same with a day. I'm always arranging and rearranging my schedule, my meals, my clothes, my free time, my people, and so on. It has taken me years to grasp that I can make all the plans I want, but circumstances beyond my control, people with or without my permission, not to mention the Lord's unrevealed plans, can disrupt my intentions.

Last spring my daughter-in-law, Danya, and I decided to tackle a few boxes in the attic of my garage. They were "leftovers" that hadn't been unpacked since our move to Tennessee two years earlier. (Which is a strong hint I didn't need what was in them.) Things were going well, just as I had planned, when a large box full of heavy dishes that was sitting atop another big box suddenly fell and landed on my right foot. This was not planned. May I just say, it hurt. But given to a deep strain of denial that runs rampant in our family line, I just kept hobbling along.

Four days later as I limped home from a walk to town, tears streaming down my face, I finally admitted to myself that I may have hurt my foot more than I thought. I went to an emergency bone clinic (didn't know those existed) where they x-rayed it, socked it, and put it in a boot cast. Seems I fractured two bones on the top of my foot.

Now to make things a tad more interesting, I was on a bus tour during that spring with my buddy Sandi Patty. So I had to decide how I would handle this painful inconvenience. I knew climbing on and off the bus with this boot that kept throwing off my balance, getting in and out of the bunk beds on the bus, and managing my stage time up and down steps could get trying. I didn't want to be Greta the Griper.

> If you don't like something, change
> it. If you can't change it, change
> your attitude.—Maya Angelou

That's when flexibility needed to come into play. I find I am the most pliable when I'm grateful instead of grumbly. So I took another look at my situation and realized that the box could have fallen on my head (much harder to boot), the breaks in my foot could have required surgery, I could have been bound in an old plaster cast instead of the new Velcro boot that was removable for bathing, and it was easier to ride the bus than to go through security lines at the airport.

Through gratitude's lens I was able to align my heart with a pliable attitude, which I'm certain pleased God. I could—and have, in other circumstances—complained my way through inconveniences, only adding to my misfortune and anyone who encountered me.

I have found flexibility to be a necessary asset if we are to survive the dailyness of life. And I don't have flex naturally. Ask anyone who knows me. When you see me flex it's because I have gotten down on my knees and asked God to help me be brave and grateful.

A lack of flex is often about fear. A realization of how little say-so we have in this big, unruly world can cause our insecurity to come forth, as well as our anger. And anger is often fear's tutu. By that I mean fear and anger wear disguises, and what looks like one can actually be the other. They're tricky that way.

If we are to decorate our day we must at times drag, pull, and lug the heavy furniture of facing the truth. And the truth is, we are not in charge. Whoever said we need to hand in our badge as director of the universe was right. Relinquishment and flexibility are kissing cousins, and gratitude is their best friend.

Here are some additional ways to decorate today and tomorrow and the following day, etc.

Sidle up to joy. Don't have any yourself? Deliberately hang with those who do. Can't think of anyone? Visit a kindergarten room. Or work in the church nursery. Those lovebugs have oodles of joy, and they share.

> Hello, sun in my face. Hello, you who
> made the morning and spread it over the
> fields . . . Watch, now, how I start the day
> in happiness, in kindness.—Mary Oliver

Give away something you value. Expect nothing in return. It will decorate your heart with a smile you can't wipe away.

> You have not lived today until you have
> done something for someone who can
> never repay you.—John Bunyan

Volunteer your services. It might be at a hospital, a food line, at a rehab center, etc. Volunteering will enhance your gratitude and remind you what matters.

> There is no exercise better for the
> heart than reaching down and lifting
> people up.—John Holmes

Use your gift. Drag it out of the closet if necessary. Your gift might be cake decorating, watercolors, singing, hospitality, etc. My friend MaryLou reads to the disabled and disadvantaged. Whatever is your "thing" . . . bless someone. God gave us gifts so that we might be extravagant toward others.

Give what you have. To someone it
may be better than you dare to think.
—Henry Wadsworth Longfellow

Unpack your gratitude. Share with others what you're thankful for. You might be surprised what you learn about yourself and God. Some gratitude comes with hindsight and can transform past pain into a purposed path. (I never imagined that my agoraphobic days would be used to help others with their troubled emotions. During the drudgery of getting well, I confess, I was not applauding my splintered condition. But today I can clearly trace God's hand in my redemption and I'm grateful that those years have taught me compassion and usefulness.)

If the only prayer you said was thank you,
that would be enough.—Meister Eckhart

Visit a senior. Let her talk. It will be cathartic for you both. I've been on both sides. Trust me, it matters.

When we give cheerfully and accept gratefully,
everyone is blessed.—Maya Angelou

Compliment a stranger. It can change the day for both of you.

For it is in giving that we receive.
—Saint Francis of Assisi

Let's sum it up. To decorate our day takes an effort on our part to rearrange what we can and leave the heavy lifting to God. It's that simple and that hard. Perhaps placing our names on the creed below will cause us to be more conscious of our daily choices. Want to sign up?

I will give up my right to rule the universe and acknowledge God's sovereignty. I will remain flexible during inconveniences and interruptions, recognizing that we live in a fallen world. I will purpose to be grateful knowing it pleases the heart of God.
Sign here please _____

1. When was the last time you had to adjust your attitude?
2. What have you stored away that you need to drag out and share?
3. What might you do to decorate today?

FIVE
read

By words the mind is winged.

—ARISTOPHANES

I know, I know. Every book I write I'm guilty of waxing loquacious about reading. I can't help myself. When something changes your life, it's human tendency, and certainly mine, to go on and on. Because let's face it, life is bursting at the seams with demands and we need reminders of what can help us bear up and press on. Or at least that's the excuse I use to say . . . *read*, please.

God used books to save my life by giving me counsel through the printed pages. I had too many ills and issues to be resolved

27

easily or quickly, so he sent books via friends to offer me small hopes, daily mercies, page-by-page kindnesses that led, like stepping stones, to big resolve.

I'll say it again: books changed my life. Why the Lord chose that vehicle for my recovery is a mystery because I was not a reader until desperation set in and I was reaching for a way out of my despair. During my phobic years books were my rope of hope. During that time I read Hannah Hurnard, Oswald Chambers, Catherine Marshall, Charles Swindoll, Dwight Moody, Hannah Whitall Smith, Jill Briscoe, etc. The list goes on.

Reading doesn't make brain cells, but it does give us something to put inside the ones we have. And we have plenty. Scientists claim we have 100 billion brain cells.[1] Talk about unused space. And were you aware that there are 151 million books in the Library of Congress on 838 miles of bookshelves?[2] That means we have enough space to hold the entire library in our head if we tucked one book into each cell, and we'd still have tons of space left over and wouldn't have to walk miles to find them. That gives new dimension to having a big head.

We've all noticed that the publishing world has gone through dramatic changes over the past few years, affecting the way we shop and read. Suddenly, we the consumer are downloading our book selections onto electronic reading devices instead of buying them at the local bookstores, which if they still exist, are now coffee shops with gift selections and a few peripheral books.

So it appears the times are gone when we could while away a day tucked in a chair with countless books at our elbow as we thumbed through the pages and made our choices. I personally found it great fun to arrive home after a day of perusing and fall face-first into a couple of well-written adventures.

I confess I do own an electronic reader, but I also have bookcases full of tomes that I can hold close, dog-ear, and write in the margins. All these activities help me retain their contents. I like to cuddle with my books. I'm very tactile. I'm won over by a book's heft, paper quality, illustrations, and font. But the main sell is the content. I've bought many an ugly book when I've heard from reliable sources that the writing was sterling.

One of those "ugly" books years ago was a slim volume by Lewis Smede titled *How Can It Be All Right When Everything Is All Wrong?*[3] An excellent volume of truth encased in a less-than-appealing cover. I knew people would overlook this valuable contribution if they judged its worth on its looks, so when I was given the opportunity to review the book for four thousand women at a Winning Women's conference, I alerted them to the cherished contents. During the break word was sent down from the bookstore that people were lining up for the "ugly book," but no one remembered the real title. Within minutes of receiving word of its identity, the book sold out.

We all long to possess the book that will help liberate us. I have found only Jesus sets prisoners free, but he uses myriad ways to accomplish his plans. For me it included books . . . with priority given to his Book.

The Bible is full of jaw-dropping, heart-rattling, head-boggling stories recorded to shake us out of complacency and lead us to the Savior. I never tire of Joseph's journey, Hannah's song, Ruth's endurance, Jonah's voyage, Paul's determination, John's visions, or

Jesus' sacrifice. The Bible helps us know God and his heart for us. That's deeply comforting.

I love to know what people are reading wherever I am. I crane my neck at airports, on planes, in hotel lobbies, and at bookstores to see what kind of books people are drawn to. Electronic readers don't have dust jackets or spines with titles on them, so it interferes with my inquisitive nature. I also like to check the latest best-seller lists to see what's hot and what's not. I love the lists of the most popular books ever written, hoping to eventually add to my own tally of accomplished reads. Some books never fall off the top charts, like *Pride and Prejudice, To Kill a Mockingbird, Alice in Wonderland,* and *Little Women,* to name a few. Have you checked those off your list yet?

I often give books as gifts . . . especially to my grandsons. When our oldest grandson, Justin, was still quite young (he's twelve now) I gave him a set of Dick and Jane books as one of his Christmas gifts. Upon opening the chubby package he rolled his eyes, dropped his shoulders, and groaned, "Books, books, books. You always give me books."

The room got quiet . . . then his mom called Justin into another room where they had a discussion, evidently a refresher course on manners, because when he returned his gratitude had improved. We would all learn a few years later, to our surprise, Justin had a reading challenge, which frustrated him and colored his view of books. So we immediately got Justin some help and today he enjoys a good read. In fact, I have a hard time keeping up with his wish list. Yea!

I'm told the average person reads fewer than one book per year. Please tell me it isn't so.

> You don't have to burn books to
> destroy a culture. Just get people to
> stop reading them.—Ray Bradbury

It is a proven fact we are better conversationalists when we read. Our vocabularies are more expansive and our word choices tend to be charged with meaning. People are more likely to seek us out as good company. We are more likely to be promoted in the workplace. Books remind us we are not alone in our struggles, and they can help us to evaluate our own needs more objectively. And the list goes on.

> Not all readers are leaders, but all leaders
> are readers.—Harry S. Truman

For me a good read is one that allows me to come to my own conclusions and doesn't try to strong-arm me into the author's position. If it's a piece of fiction, I like a substantial work that doesn't find it necessary to riddle the story with expletives to show muscle. Books are meant to companion us. I like a book that invites me in, treats me with respect, and one I can exit with my integrity still intact.

What about you?

1. Why do you read?
2. What authors speak your language?
3. Why are books great gifts?

SIX

rest

He makes me lie down in green pastures.

—PSALM 23:2

My dad had the gift of nap. I mean, he had napping down to a college course. He loved teaching it by demonstration. The most important possession he owned to implement his gift was his recliner—aka his BFF (best friend forever). His second requirement was a newspaper. Not to read. Oh no, it became a tent that he filled with his radical snoring, which made it rise and fall more often than the stock market. It didn't look comfortable to be sucking the sports section in and out your nostrils, but hey, different strokes for different folks. It sure worked for him. Then he had to remove his shoes. It comforted him after a long day of delivering milk to take his work boots off. But it also made him vulnerable because he was extremely ticklish and his long, narrow stocking feet were a target for impish children (yes, me). Just saying the words "tickle, tickle" in his presence was not in anyone's best interest (I couldn't help myself).

So with chair tipped back, paper tent constructed, and feet pointed toward Jupiter the nap would proceed, followed quickly by the worst snoring you've ever heard. I kid you not: earthworms would rise up out of the ground in fear, mothers would call their children indoors, and dogs for miles would pace and yelp. That man had a gift that would make your tutu twirl.

> People who snore always fall
> asleep first.—Anonymous

Who knew that years later there would be so many advocates touting a nap's medicinal value? My dad would have felt so justified, especially since we, his family, teased him unmercifully about being such a noisy napaholic. Today he would have been a man ahead of his time.

After Dad died my mom picked up napping where he left off. Except Mom was a quiet napper and could sit up straight and doze off only to wake up and then do it all over again. Now I've become a napper and my style is like my mom's—except on occasion I snort myself awake. Very unladylike, but entertaining I'm sure to passengers on my same flights.

Napping is not new, but it seems to go in and out of popularity. Leonardo da Vinci took multiple naps and then slept less at night. I get that. Napoleon, Edison, and Churchill were all avid nappers. Eleanor Roosevelt would nap before speeches to boost her energy. (If I spoke right after a nap I'd be loopier than I already am. It takes me a while to throw off my nap groggies.)

Many of my friends, all much younger, are now nap conscious. Some take power naps for seven to twelve minutes, while others reserve at least thirty minutes out of their day for renewal. I must admit it's addictive and the body seems more than willing to support the habit, which may indicate our need. We were designed to work hard and rest well. I think our society has the hard work down, but sleeping well at night seems to be the impossible dream.

We are a medicated nation. And taking sleep aids is at an all-time high. It is estimated that some seventy million people have a sleep problem. I wonder if it's because so much of our work today is done indoors and requires a chair and a monitor. I love the idea of these new standing desks so at least we can change positions and allow the blood to flow. Also many companies make exercise equipment available for break time because they believe it adds to the productivity of their employees.

I live in a community of bikers, runners, and walkers. I really do think outdoor activities help us sleep better, so I try to walk to town regularly (two blocks) and fiddle with my tiny potted garden at home. I do think our sleep needs for optimum function are different according to age, physical condition, and activities. I've been reading up on health reports on why our sleep is imperative, and here's what I've learned.

Sleep restores optimum brain function. Okay, now that appeals to me. My brain used to be like a cup—it actually held information. Now it's more like a sieve. So I need optimum function. Churchill believed his naps helped him get twice as much done.

Get this: it is suggested that not sleeping well at night adds to weight gain. Well, yes, because I'm awake raiding the frozen grapes. Duh.

Sleep helps our immune system fight off disease. My nutritionist told me years ago at bedtime to soak my feet in very warm water, dry them, slip them into socks, and climb into bed. That shot of blood flow would assist my immune system in taking care of repair work it needed to do while I was sleeping. Besides, I found until my feet are warm I can't fall asleep.

Experts believe that sleep helps with irritability and moods. Wait till my hubby hears that . . . he'll send me right to bed. I admit there is something about a good night's sleep that improves my attitude. I feel better prepared to take on the day . . . and to be sweet.

If it's true that sleep improves creativity, I'm all over that. I think being creative is one of the primary ways we become like Jesus. There's something about capturing a sunset, hosting a dinner, designing a house, or writing a poem that aligns us with his creative nature. What a privilege it is to join him in adding beauty to the world!

Honestly, as I age my sleep patterns have become more unpredictable. I'm finding it takes a lot more discipline to set myself up for sleep. Resisting sweets, ice cream, and chocolate after six o'clock seems helpful. And personally I can't handle any caffeine after three, which includes chocolate; otherwise I'm practicing Zumba steps at midnight, which tends to annoy Les. Reading soothing books in the evening or watching a home-and-garden show instead of getting tied up in a suspense drama on television helps me too.

The Bible mentions sleep often. Here are two of my favorite verses for very different reasons:

> When Jacob awoke from his sleep,
> he thought, "Surely the LORD is in this
> place, and I was not aware of it."
> —Genesis 28:16 NIV

When I'm rested I am far more likely to discern God's presence and not give in to ragtag emotions as I wrestle with my problems and fears.

> The captain went to [Jonah] and said, "How
> can you sleep? Get up and call on your god!"
> —Jonah 1:6 NIV

While our sleep is God-given, we also can use it in an attempt to escape so we don't have to face God or others. I slept away a good part of my young adult life so I didn't have to feel the weight of my sadness. A healthy night's sleep is six to nine hours—more for growing children or those recovering from surgery or illness. If you are always tired, have a doctor check your thyroid and your vitamin D levels. Beyond that, seek counsel. Be proactive. It's a sign of maturity when we reach out for help.

I asked my friend Karen Anderson to write you a poem about sleep. The result is a picture of all that pokes and prods at us while we try to make peace with our pillow.

Now I Lay Me Down To Sleep . . .

Some days easier said than done
longing for rest and peace and quiet
days, weeks, years of mind-whirling
running, pleasing, caring

Evening bedtime sounds
sometimes so loud the room feels
alive with daytime
even when it's not

Clock ticking, alarm set
with tones jarring enough to wake
from exhaustion and worry and fear

Wanting to sleep deeply, restoringly
but wondering if a little voice will call out
in the middle of the night with a fever

Or the phone that can't be turned all the way off
will ring with a call from the hospital
or nursing home, or police

Oh, Lord, did you have days like that?
when you went to lay your head down
did comfort come so readily?

Can that comfort be mine?

Calming my heart, caressing my mind
Like a tender massage working out the knots
from the pressure points of life

The voices begin to quiet
not silent, never silent
but fading as I begin to relax in the knowledge

You are with me in the darkness
as you slept in the darkness
trusting your Father was ever present.

So now I lay me down to sleep . . .
I pray the Lord my soul to keep.

KAREN ANDERSON

Our Shepherd never slumbers, so sleep,
sweet sheep. You're safe in his care.
—Patsy Clairmont

1. How many hours of sleep do you average a night?
2. What are nighttime rituals that help you settle down?
3. Is there a Psalm that comforts you at night?

SEVEN

wings

Oh, that I had the wings of a dove!

—Psalm 55:6

Did you know that there are zebra doves? No, you can't ride them; they are doves that look like zebras in that they sport a striped jammies look. Zebras with wings—that makes me giggle. And there are whistling doves (guess they got bored with cooing); and get this, there are eared doves. Who knew?

Doves and pigeons are categorized together because there is very little difference between them, if any. Usually doves are a tad smaller. These two birds range from the size of a sparrow to the size of a turkey. A turkey? I love God's flourish in creation. (Although I must admit I would be startled to see a pigeon the size of a turkey on my front stoop. Talk about needing a pooper scooper and a car wash!)

What should really interest us about the Bible verse above is the dove's wings. They are large. A dove's wing muscles alone constitute 31 to 44 percent of its body weight.[1] Think of it: wouldn't it be great if to lose almost half our weight all we had to do was shed our wings until we needed them? We could hang them out to air and only don them at flight time. That makes my heart flutter.

Pigeons and doves are among the strongest fliers of all birds. Maybe that's why they show up all over the globe. And dove wings are highly maneuverable, which explains their aerial ability. They make their way around congested cities and perch on precarious windowsills, billboards, and statues, while dodging pedestrians, light poles, dogs, and traffic. Talk about twirling!

As a kid I dreamed of flying, but then who hasn't? Not in an airplane, but free flight—arms stretched, toes pointed . . . *whoosh*. A video was on the news the other night of children jumping from a rooftop into a snow bank. Dangerous and crazy, yes, but for three to four seconds they felt the exhilaration of flight. What fun! I wonder if the lure of exhilaration is what got the Wright brothers looking skyward?

I am a frequent flier with several airlines. I have been flying back and forth across the country for thirty-eight years. I think I deserve a set of wings beyond the lapel ones in my jewelry box. What time it would save me if I could walk out my front door, lift off, and land at my destination! Of course, I'd need an insulated flight suit, a GPS, a lightning deflector, a weather scanner, a radar, and a valet to carry my luggage. Hm, perhaps I'd better just board a 737 and leave the flying to the pilot.

> Oh, that I had the wings of a dove!
> I would fly away and be at rest.
> *I would flee far away . . .*
> —Psalm 55:6–7 NIV

This verse is about someone who wants to escape. I get that. Don't you? There are just days when life is too hard and people too problematic, when wings seem like the solution. Days when the husband doesn't "get us," the kids aren't listening, our friends are unavailable, and the toilet won't stop running. When we lose our job, our funds are depleted, and our church has split.

I have found when I stay grounded, understanding by God's sovereign design this too will pass, and trudge my way through the pain and hardship, I am lifted. Lifted by the Lord's morning-by-morning compassion and by an understanding of God's constancy and companionship in the midst of heartbreak.

My closest friend died from cancer. I was devastated, and I still battle bouts of melancholy. Carol's illness was a painful journey, and her death has been a cruel boundary between us. Those of us who loved her understand she is with Jesus, but we miss her dear presence with us. Is that selfish? Perhaps, but that doesn't change our longing. Gratefully, she left a legacy that we take comfort in— it's a legacy of wings.

Carol knew how to lift people's spirits. She did it in many ways.

Carol battled shyness all her life, but she didn't allow that to stop her from being kind, generous, artistic, and loving. Her quiet offerings were hard to miss because she was a great cook, a merciful giver, and a compassionate listener. Think of it: she would feed you great food, laugh at your jokes, tenderly care for your wounds, and look at you while you talked. Now you have to admit, that's rare.

Carol was a dedicated wife and mom, a delightful friend, and a devoted follower of Christ. She was a spectacular artist who splashed color on all she did: the way she dressed, decorated her home, set a table, and celebrated her grandchildren. And because of all these qualities she was, as you can imagine, popular with all who met her.

I know that people wax eloquent about folks who have died, but honestly I would have told you the same things while Carol was living. Her gentleness alone in life's harsh environment was so inviting and comforting. It wasn't that she had no faults; it was that her strengths were so mercifully defined they overshadowed her frailty.

Carol and I shared brain-twirls, but somehow ditzy on her was endearing. She made us laugh . . . a lot, and she didn't even mean to. Carol always laughed along with us; she didn't take herself too seriously. Carol regularly was caught in predicaments that left us scratching our heads and slapping our knees. I'll never know how she got out of the driver's seat with the key still in the ignition, while it was in gear and moving—and then was surprised as it drove away without her. My friend often had her head in the clouds and her wings tangled, like a kite, in the branches of a tree.

Carol reminded us by her example to love little things: a kitten's breath, frosting on a cupcake, a baby's pudgy hand, a pin on a lapel, the form of a cloud, the colors in a petal, the breeze that caused curtains to dance, a child's art, and the finishing touches on a meal.

I miss my friend. I will, I'm sure, till glory. And when I need wings, I think of the way God designed Carol with such artsy flair and tender praise, and I feel my spirits lift. Her legacy of kindness reminds me why we are here: to honor God and respect each other. Carol had an admirable way of encountering people and leaving their dignity intact, and even enhanced. We were dear friends for more than fifty years, and she never, in all those years, said a cross word to me. Imagine that. I thank God for putting Carol in my life on the first day of seventh grade. She was scared and I thought I was taking her under my tough wings, but it would be Carol who would shelter me in her tender graces.

> Oh, that I had the wings of a dove!
> I would fly away and be at rest.
> I would flee far away
> *And stay in the desert.*
> —Psalm 55:6–7 NIV

As good as escaping might sound, we weren't meant to stay in the desert. We would soon grow weary of sagebrush and isolation. Our spirits would wilt. Our soul would parch. We were meant to live in community, as hard at times as that can be. To survive each other and our losses and learn to flourish, we will need wings . . . not to escape but to lift and be lifted by wafts of encouragement.

Growing wings, I believe, is a matter of allowing God to use the strength he's given to us and allowing God to convert our humanity into joy. And he taught me through my friend to lean into others, not so much with answers, but with a listening ear to let them know they are heard. To be intentionally kind.

Kindness never loses its charm. And when kindness is mixed with mercy you have a healing balm, causing others to seek you out. I am reminded to be gentle with people's feelings; their emotions don't have to agree with mine. Our goal is not to align people with who we are but to love them toward who Christ is, and he'll handle the rest. Yes, he will handle the rest.

Until glory . . . fly high and land soft. There are a cloud of witnesses cheering us on.

1. When was the last time you wished you could fly away? Why?
2. Do you take yourself too seriously? If so, how can you rise above it?
3. Who extends kindness with mercy to you? Have you thanked them?

laugh

Laughter is the shortest distance between two people.

—Victor Borge

My husband, Les, has an electric cart he drives to town because his legs are no longer reliable to hold him steady. His cart is a zippy one because he's a dart-and-dash type of fellow. So recently, when our town had a celebration with lots of food carts and booths, he jumped on his cart and scooted through the crowd like a bee headed for a patch of sunflowers. I eventually ambled my way to the gathering and visited a few of my favorite shops, and when I didn't spot Les, I traipsed back home.

A short time later Les boogied home and announced he had eaten the best crackers of his life at one of the tents. He held up a small bag and then set them down by the coffeepot. He tried to tempt me with one, but I had just finished a fish taco and couldn't have choked down a toothpick. I could see he was disappointed that I wasn't going to share in his new find. (I mean, how good could a cracker be anyway?)

Later, as I was walking through the kitchen, my eyes caught a glimpse of the bag, so I thought I'd test the crackers. It looked like an ordinary whole wheat cracker, so I couldn't imagine what was so special. I crunched down on it and was immediately displeased with how dry it was. Then the flavor hit my taste buds and it was close to disgusting. I stood there startled that my husband thought these were a great discovery. Then I thought maybe I was judging too quickly, so I put another cracker in my mouth only to be quickly reminded how bad they were. Les walked in the kitchen and saw my face all twisted as I struggled to swallow the final bite.

"What are you doing?" he asked, looking puzzled.

"I just ate one of your great crackers, thank you very much. They are terrible," I emphasized.

"Honey, those aren't the crackers I liked. Those are for the dog."

Excuse me?

I had eaten two dog crackers . . . not one, but two.

Uno. Dos.

We don't even have a dog!

Who buys crackers for their grand-dog?

My husband, evidently.

I growled the rest of the day.

Honestly, if you don't laugh at life's awkward twists and turns, you will growl and possibly bite. I am convinced God created us with the capacity to laugh to give us a way to survive the quirky things that happen. Plus, it's a great way to unload overtaxed emotions.

Laughter is an instant vacation.—Milton Berle

How often do you long for a vacation? Just think: we have mini ones at our constant disposal. Lighten up, look for the fun, and laugh yourself happy.

We've probably all read the health benefits of laughter until it's not funny anymore, but in case you've forgotten here's a reminder. I reiterate because our forgetter forgets when life intensifies, which is when we need laughter the most. To make my point *Psychology Today* reports, "Five-year-olds laugh 300 times a day. The average adult? Only four."[1]

Now that's startling.

Laughter. It improves our overall sense of well-being. When I speak at Women of Faith conferences the comment I hear most often is, "Thank you for making me laugh. I really needed that." When we guffaw we can literally feel the stress run out of us in tears and tension.

Laughter. It builds relationships. We can be in a room full of strangers and have a good group laugh only to find we now feel relaxed and connected, allowing an opportunity for new friend-ships to open up naturally. Or we can be cranky with a mate, friend, or coworker. Then, after a good chortle our attitude and theirs over-come the dispute so we can move on amiably.

Laughter. Even a smile, the beginning of laughter, communicates approachability, hospitality, and friendliness. I have heard that DJs often have mirrors in the studio to remind themselves to smile while on the air because it's proven they sound friendlier.

Laughter. It is an emotional clearinghouse and therefore brings relief.

Laughter. I'm told it lowers blood pressure and increases blood flow. I'm no doctor, but it makes sense that tension would pinch our blood flow while laughter would open our arteries.

It's like knowing we should drink half our weight in water every day, yet if you are like me you're lucky if you drink your shoe size. Most of us get so caught up in life's challenges we don't take care of ourselves.

> Mirth is God's medicine. Everybody ought
> to bathe in it.—Henry Ward Beecher

Recently I had to have an ultrasound on my gallbladder and liver. When I arrived in the room with the gal who would perform the test she said something to me about excusing her, but she had her back to me and her voice was muffled, so I didn't quite catch what I was supposed to excuse . . . until she sat down next to me. The poor dear had the hiccups. Not little delicate ones, but ones that caused her whole body to quake in seismic spasms. It became quite interesting when she'd position the monitor on my gallbladder region and try to take the picture; then invariably she would have a surge of hiccup spasms that caused the monitor to jolt upward. The technician was trying to be professional and pretend it wasn't happening, and I was trying not to giggle. She'd reposition the monitor when, sure enough, another jolt of hiccups would send it skidding to other parts of my anatomy.

Gratefully, the test was short and I shot out of there. On the ride home I told my daughter-in-law, who had driven me, what had happened. We laughed all the way home. It wasn't funny the tech was uncomfortable, but what was hilarious to me was thinking of the person who would read my test. Don't you know they wondered how my tonsils ended up in my gallbladder and how a breast could be growing out of my liver? I didn't have the heart to laugh in the girl's presence because I could see she was embarrassed, but honestly it could happen to anyone.

Life is full of hiccups . . . and dog biscuits, so we might as well laugh. To share the moment with someone else just doubles the pleasure.

1. When is the last time you laughed until you cried?
2. Do you need a laugh vacation? If so, how can you help that happen?
3. When something's funny, who is the first person you want to tell? Why?

ponder

Work is not always required. There is such a thing as sacred idleness.

—George MacDonald

Why do you think God has to lead us to still waters? Why don't we willingly toss our sketch pad and Bible in a backpack and head for a quiet stream? Why does he have to tell us repeatedly to be still, to be quiet, and to rest? You'd think we'd know to do this.

A friend stopped by today and said, "I can't stay, but I wanted to hug your neck and then I have to run. Sorry that I haven't been a better friend, but I've been so busy."

She reminded me of the rabbit in *Alice in Wonderland*. You know, the one with the oversized pocket watch who is always running late and murmuring about his obligations. And my friend wasn't saying anything that I'm not guilty of myself. I have good intentions that are chewed up and spit out by my other twirling demands.

As a kid I actually remember being bored. Now I pray for bored. Not a lifelong bored, but say, a week. Or a day. This whirlpool of activity that we seem to share has all but erased leisurely porch-swing conversations. Or slow ambles through a park where you take time to examine a leaf or pull petals from a flower. Or a long lunch, chewing on things that matter. Or an extended, knee-bending talk with the Lord.

How long has it been since you lingered over verses from Scripture, allowing God to write them on your heart's tablet?

Twenty-five years ago I remember reading and rereading a book by Evelyn Christenson, *Lord, Change Me.*[1] It taught a personalized, meditative study style. I'm not surprised the book is still in print because it's such a valuable, applicable, and timeless message. The part that has stayed with me is where Evelyn instructs the reader to start reading a portion of Scripture until something stops you. A word. A principle. Conviction. Unsettledness. Then you stay with that verse(s) for as long as it takes to absorb what the Lord is trying to say to you.

I found that so helpful. It put brakes on my speeding brain. It is my style to read fast and press on. But this approach puts the emphasis on being more sensitive to God's leading—to pay attention and inspect every word, then stop and mentally absorb what's being said or what's being asked. I thought I was doing that in my own skittering way, but when I deliberately slowed down I became aware of my need to linger and to pray over verses intentionally. Evelyn's insights inspired my approach.

Being meditative can protect us from society's hype. How many of us own a smartphone? (Me.) A fancy one-cup-at-a-time coffeepot? (Yep.) An undergarment that squeezes our waist muffin up into our tonsils? (Uh-huh.) We all want to fit in, not just our clothes but each other's standards. But God's ways are so different from our natural leanings. For instance, the Lord asks us to "love your [our] enemies" (Matthew 5:44). Hm, personally I need help to love people I care about, so what are the chances I'm going to love my enemies? It won't happen without God's intervention. He tells us, "Do good to those who hate you" (Matthew 5:44). Really? We tend to be a retaliatory people, which is why our courts and prisons are bursting at the bars. Because we have our rights. Right?

I need divine reminders of who I am and how I am to be. Daily is not too often. Today's media packaging can be slick and sound oh so right. To slice through to what matters, I need Jesus. Society says ramp it up; Jesus says slow it down. Society promotes living for yourself, while Jesus calls us to think of others more highly than ourselves. We are encouraged to buy, buy, buy, but Jesus says our debts will make us slaves.

I find it noteworthy that Jesus came as a rule breaker and a peacemaker. We believe you can be one or the other, yet clearly Jesus was both. I find God, his Son, and the Spirit to be a holy mystery. The Godhead is more than worthy of our contemplation.

We can never finish exploring the depths of their identity. They cannot be hemmed in by our imaginations, opinions, or even our doctrines. No matter how well or long you have known Christ, he is more. Much more.

"Peace, be still," Christ counsels us in the midst of fear and uncertainty (Mark 4:39). This verse suggests that we must quiet ourselves if we are to grasp that God is who he says he is. And don't we need to be reassured in these troubling times? It seems world peace is threadbare, the economy is precarious, and our personal security is constantly under the threat of the next person to purchase a semiautomatic weapon. Yes, I long for a quiet center.

> Sometimes I need only to stand wherever
> I am to be blessed.—Mary Oliver

I can delude myself into thinking I have to "get away" if I'm to meditate. But truly I find the greatest racket is inside me, and I tend to be my biggest distraction as well. Not the phone or doorbell (which is still playing Christmas songs in April), or housework calling my name (I considered changing it), but noisy, head-clanging me. I have head racket and an undisciplined attention span. I think it's splintered from multitasking. I don't need a monastery to meditate any more than I need a rippling brook, crashing waves, or mountain breezes. They'd be lovely, oh yes, they would, but truly not necessary. What I need is increased desire and practiced discipline. Now add to that when possible brooks, waves, and breezes . . . and the package sweetens. But I find when I am faithful in the midst of the fray to seek Christ, I have a greater sense of his nearness, his companionship, his peace.

Desire: to long for.
Discipline: a regimen that develops a skill

Meditation is not all about what we do, but when we mentally position ourselves to listen for God's voice, I believe he will do the rest. We hear him in a thought, a verse, a prompting. Not an audible voice, but internally and visually through creation. And when we reflect upon his word, truth will rise to meet us.

I don't always hear his voice during meditation, but often it will be later in the day during a conversation with a friend when a verse I gleaned in the quiet will rise up to meet the noise in her life. There's something so deeply personal when God allows us to be the one to deliver his message of love.

Sweet are the thoughts that savor
of content; the quiet mind is richer
than a crown.—Robert Greene

As I grow older I seek the shelter of silence more and more. When I was younger I would flip on the television or music as background when I was alone. But now, given the option, I turn off everything. It allows the quiet to settle inside my ruffled places, inside the voices of the day, and hushes them. I need the quiet to balance the frenetic in my life. I need the quiet to discern Christ's voice from all the others. It's then I am still enough to remember what matters, to settle my disputes with God and others, and to feed my soul truth that offers me a future and a hope.

1. Name a peaceful setting that you've been to.
2. Do you have a quiet space in your home?
3. How do you think quiet helps you?
4. Do a study on the words *quiet*, *still*, and *peace*. Record what you learn.

T E N

pen

Of all the attitudes we can acquire, surely the attitude of gratitude is the most important and by far the most life-changing.

—Zig Ziglar

Did you know a ballpoint pen can write approximately forty-five thousand words before it runs dry?[1] But it needs help to accomplish its potential. In this techno-world we live in, the pen seems almost passé. It's not that we never need it, but we need it far less than we once did.

I don't know about you, but I receive very few handwritten letters anymore. It's all e-mails, texts, tweets, Facebook posts,

Instagram pictures, and phone messages. I confess I love the convenience they afford and the time they save. Yet when the rare handwritten envelope does show up in my fistful of junk mail, it is with great interest that I peruse it. I check to see if I recognize the person's handwriting, because there's something so personal about our script: the tilt of our *t*'s, the loop of our *y*'s, the flying dots on our *i*'s, and the size of our letters, for instance.

I always knew my mamaw's handwriting because it left the letters quivering, like they had slept out in the cold. My brother printed. Small print. Actually tiny. My dad had a twirling *S* for his first name Smith (yes, Smith), and he always included in his signature his middle initial *W* for Waller (yes, Waller). The rest of his name was almost illegible. But because he was consistent with his scrawl, it was recognizable to those of us who knew him. My mom's writing was tidy. Just like her. She had a distinctive *R* for Rebecca. It was chubby.

Even though they all died years ago, I have retained scraps of their writing. It's sweet when I am glancing through an old box of photographs and I happen across a letter from my mamaw, a card signed by my brother, an old report card signed by my mom, or a document signed by my dad. I see their penmanship and instantly recognize them as if I'd seen their picture. It warms my heart.

Now I mention that to say this: even though our busy lives crowd us to the fence, can you think of someone who would be blessed to have your handwriting in her mailbox? Someone who would think enough of it that she would slip it in a chest and reread it again and again? I love personal notes, especially from people with whom I have a shared history.

When I was a child, my grandmother kept her letters tied in bundles tucked inside an old gnarly trunk. It's still such a dear memory. I'd watch her pull out a bundle—some tied with yarn, others held with elastic—and then she'd wiggle a letter from the stack to read to me. You could tell Mamaw had read them many times because they were creased with her scrutiny as she held them to the light to make sure she hadn't missed a single word.

Mamaw kept a store-bought tablet and a ballpoint pen in her trunk for the moments when she would compose a letter. It was quite an ordeal for Mamaw to pen a letter with her shaded house, her poor vision, and her second-grade education. She was self-taught, and Mamaw worked hard to advance herself. I wish I would have told her how proud I am of her achievements. I'm not sure I even realized what she had done to make a life for herself and her family until after she passed. My grandmother never made any fuss over herself.

Speaking of making a fuss, I just read about one of the most beautiful and expensive pens in the world. Two thousand encrusted diamonds and a gold nib adorn it. Get this: it cost one million, four hundred seventy-two thousand dollars. Now if that doesn't dry up the ink in your refill, I don't know what will. It sure makes you rethink the answer to, "May I borrow your pen?"

Only one of those creations is designed each year, making it highly desirable. I wonder what my mamaw would think of that, she who collected her table dishes free from boxes of oatmeal?

I think the folks involved in the signing of the Declaration of Independence had the right idea. They used an eagle feather quill for the signing. Scale a mountain and pluck a feather out of a nest and it's a done deal. Cost: two bandages and a backpack. That's more in my budget.

One of the most famous names on the Declaration was John Hancock, whose very name later became interchangeable with the word *signature*. "Put your John Hancock right there," we tell folks when we need them to sign something. I bet John would be surprised.

I'm into documents. Family documents. I have a postcard from 1918 from the War Department to my grandfather, I have my grandparents' school tax receipts from 1938 to 1958, I have a War Ration Book sent to my dad in the 1930s, etc. I have the dog tag of my uncle who was killed in World War II, before I was born. The family received the Purple Heart for his service.

Along with old documents I've kept thank-you notes that have been especially meaningful through the years. There's just something about expressed gratitude that is memorable and endearing. We all like to be thanked when we have gone out of our way to be helpful or thoughtful. Their acknowledgment tells us we made our goal of being a meaningful part of their life and celebration.

I came across a birthday card that my dearest friend Carol sent me years ago. Inside was her warm, artistic handwriting expressing her appreciation for our friendship. She died five years ago, but honestly, when I came across that card and read her words, it felt like we had a bona fide teacup visit. We had been friends for over fifty years and had written many notes to each other. Wish I had them all now.

Do you express your gratitude readily? It's so healthy. I read somewhere that you cannot be afraid and grateful at the same time. You can be one or the other. That's great news because it means the next time we are fearful we can use gratitude to obliterate scary feelings and thoughts. That's huge.

> Be anxious for nothing, but in everything by prayer and supplication, with thanksgiving, let your requests be made known to God; and the peace of God, which surpasses all understanding, will guard your hearts and minds through Christ Jesus.—Philippians 4:6–7

Developing a habit of gratitude seems well worth our time, and handwritten notes seem like an honorable effort. You might consider beginning with written prayers telling God what you are grateful for . . .

Dear God . . . this morning I woke with the warmth of the sun on my pillow and the sound of a single sparrow singing about the new day. Thank you. I know life is a gift. And I recognize you are the Gift Giver. Forgive me when I dash off into my hours and forget to acknowledge all you do. Your unfailing mercies, your lit path, your counsel, your companionship, and your daily provisions do not go unnoticed. Thank you.

And then once you get the rhythm, spread the thank-yous . . .

Dear Friend,
I'm not sure how long it has been since I have told you how much you mean to me, so I'm sure it's time. I know God had our paths

cross so I might experience more of his kindness through you. Your quiet ways remind me often of my need to not be so drama-bound. Your quick smile reminds me of what little effort it takes to brighten someone's day. And your patience with me stirs my need to extend that to others. So thank you, thank you.

It doesn't have to be long, as in forty-five thousand words—just a note will do. I have chalkboards throughout our home where I post notes of congratulations, welcome, and appreciation. Find ways to acknowledge others and observe the power of thank-you.

P.S. Today I received two handwritten thank-you notes in the mail. I was first startled and then deeply blessed. Don't think your written gratitude doesn't matter . . . trust me, it does.

1. Do you find it easy or hard to express gratitude?
2. How are you aware of God in your hours?
3. Who was the last person to send you a handwritten note? Did you answer him or her?

ELEVEN

art

Art enables us to find ourselves and lose ourselves at the same time.

—THOMAS MERTON

I can't believe it. No, you don't understand, I really can't believe it. I'm painting pictures that are identifiable. Did you hear me? You can actually tell what they are. Prior to the last few months, my stick figures had been rushed repeatedly into ICU for reconstructive surgery. And even after physical therapy they had a decided limp.

I've been trying to be an artist since childhood. I even have proof; I have projects from kindergarten. Yep, they're old all right. One of them has a dog I painted—at least, I think it's a dog, but it's the length of a cruise ship. I'm still not good at perspective..

When my friend Gail asked me if I wanted to take an art class, I immediately said yes, but later I thought, *What have I done?* It's not that I've never tried to draw and paint; it's that I've never succeeded. No matter how hard I tried. Not even a little. In fact, the last instructor I had, following our classes, sold her shop and stopped teaching. I kept telling myself not to take it personally. I'm sure I was her last straw.

And then last December my current instructor, Dorcey, came into my life and gave me a challenge and permission to find my way onto the canvas from inside of myself. This helped me with the initial hurdle of getting something onto the canvas because I tended to knot up when I tried to paint from a prescribed picture. My perfectionism of trying to paint it exactly like the photograph would block my progress. Somehow pulling from inside helped me circle around the picky-critic voice in my head.

In the beginning Dorcey didn't tell us anything we should do unless we asked her because she didn't want to interfere with our innate style while it was in the process of being defined. What a gift her permission afforded me. It increased my confidence and set me on a new creative course. One that is bringing me great delight.

Leonardo da Vinci claimed everyone can draw. I truly felt like I was the exception to that rule. But then I learned that it wasn't that I couldn't draw; it was that I couldn't see. So my drawing teacher, Melanie, began to show me new ways to look at things by seeing them as individual shapes instead of a familiar form. So a peasant woman became a collection of circles, triangles, squares, and so on. She also helped me become aware of negative spaces and their impact on our ability to see. I'm still not a good drawer, but I am better than I've ever been, which feels like respectable progress. Also, I'm learning to see life more fully.

I read somewhere that our willingness to enter our uncertainty could lead us to greater creativity. Well, trust me, when I walked into both my drawing and painting classes, I was uncertain. Like a child the first day of school, but in the weeks to follow as my confidence grew, it gradually became less scary and much more about investigative fun. It became less about the art and more about my growth. Less about my insecurity and more about steps toward maturity. Less about my perfectionism and more about acceptance of the process.

This experience has left me wanting to shout from the rooftops to those who have believed they can't, that they can. I'm not saying we'll be producing Monets, Cassatts, or Homers, but I am saying when we give ourselves permission to develop beyond where we are now, it happens. We tend to limit ourselves. Others can limit us. But in Christ we become limitless because of his provisions. God wants us to grow. He is our parent. And like any parent he is pleased when we take even wobbly steps.

Our friends Paige and Ben posted a video of their son, Asher, taking his first steps. It was exciting, and I'm not even a relative. Honestly, to watch those unsteady steps toward his mom made me tear up. I guess because I realized that it was the beginning of the world opening up for Asher. I wonder if that's how our heavenly Father feels about us when we attempt shaky steps of maturity.

In the beginning God created . . . and he has made us after his own kind that we might be creators. He's destined us to design. To make things beautiful—whether that's the landscape on the dinner table, a scrumptious menu, our home's decor, our hairstyle, an orderly pantry, or our ability to make people feel at ease.

I have a friend who makes textured journals. Another friend, Stephanie, throws her own pottery. One makes ruffled aprons. And one teaches cooking classes to kindergarteners (aw). My husband's art is stained-glass garden stones. These are all creative processes that align us with the Creator.

Art is a safe place to lower our anxiety because there's something calming about creating. Perhaps that is why at the end of each day during creation God said, ". . . and it was good."

Art is its own form of therapy. And your artistic result can be therapy for others. There's nothing I enjoy more than meandering through an art museum. It invigorates me. I sit and soak in the gifts of others. Their imagination, their color palettes, the myriad styles, and the wonder of turning a corner and having my breath catch at the sheer beauty of a painting. The intense eyes of Renoir, the dancing stars of Van Gogh, Monet's lily pads, and Homer's beach scenes are all worthy of our viewing. And that's just for starters.

> The aim of art is to represent not the
> outward appearance of things, but
> their inward significance.—Aristotle

The Metropolitan Museum of Art calendar on February 8 features the Edgar Degas oil painting *A Woman Ironing*. Ironing is such an ordinary activity, yet there is something so beautiful about this rendering that I kept returning to it again and again. Maybe it's the movement he somehow caught in her wrist, the slant of her shoulder as she leans into the task, or her meager surroundings? I'm not sure, but it's mesmerizing. As a child I saw my mom coax wrinkles out of curtains and shirts for hours on end, so maybe the common task rings with sweet familiarity. There is a dignity to what we do when we press beauty into the pages of our stories where even the daily tasks take on loveliness.

I hope you'll research this Degas picture in an art book or on the Internet and sit with it for a while. Pondering a piece will enhance your experience. Trace the story within the picture with your eyes. Is her story familiar? Do you think she loves what she is doing, or has it become drudgery? Does she seem lonely or at peace?

And now, what about you? Is your life tedious? Are you grateful for common tasks? Do you find a song in the rhythm of repetition? If Degas painted you doing a chore what would you be doing? And what would he capture? Gracefulness? Resentment?

> The purpose of art is washing the dust of
> daily life off our souls.—Pablo Picasso

Do you see how quickly art can become therapy? And therapy can become art. For me, even the movement of my paint-laden palette knife across a blank canvas, or the mixing of a paint color as cerulean blue merges into cobalt, or the finishing touches to a storm-laden cloud, all have therapeutic value.

Take it from a well-seasoned twirler . . . art yourself. Delve and discover. Find a fresh palette to help you tell your story. Try a pen, a paintbrush, a lump of clay, a journal, a floral design . . . the choices are endless. Art is often a place God uses to help us get over ourselves and find ourselves. What a dichotomy we are. What a fine piece of art!

1. When was the last time you painted a picture? What was it of? Did you like it?
2. Can you think of a time when someone gave you permission that became a turning point in your life?
3. Do you believe art is therapy? Why or why not?

TWELVE

snap

For me, the camera is a sketch book, an instrument of
intuition and spontaneity.

—Henri Cartier-Bresson

When I was a kid, I loved to jitterbug. Today, not so
much. My jitter done bugged. What I now love is being a shutter-
bug. I have a picture passion. It's less vigorous than jittering. More
productive . . . in an artsy way. I like that.

I'm not a good memory-album kind of gal. My style is more to
stuff pictures in a trunk, drawer, and closet, and then take them
out every few months and stuff them back in the drawer. No, I'm

not recommending that; I'm confessing. I have my old pictures, my mom's really old pictures, and my mamaw's ancient pictures. Of course, years ago nobody identified the folks or locations in their photographs, so many remain a mystery. And quite honestly some of the unknown (and a few of the identifiable) are scary. I mean, what's with the no smiling in pictures long ago? Golly, cheer up, people. I'm relieved we've come a long way since corsets strangled out joy and folks were doomsday stern.

Recently (day before yesterday) my friend Illy gifted me with a spunky bright red camera. It matches my glasses. I love when life complements itself. My camera is a nifty little number, and I can hardly wait to annoy people with it. Actually, I really like to take pictures of food. No kidding. It's so colorful, and when presented well it's an imaginative design of color and form. I like to try to capture the beauty of the outdoors from butterflies, to blossoms, to birds, to billowing clouds. I also enjoy well-appointed stores that display their offerings in unexpected ways, and with permission I click away. And sometimes I capture people, but usually they are unruly, and then my tolerance splinters, and I begin looking for compliant fruit bowls.

There are many scenes in Scripture I wish I could have snapped . . . like Moses and the bush. Wouldn't that have been a hot ticket on Twitter? I mean, who has seen a bush burn yet not be consumed? I bet even *National Geographic* would have paid to get a copy of that one. Or what about Abraham's goat? Joseph's coat? Noah's boat? The iron that could float? *Snap, snap, snap, snap.*

A good snapshot stops a moment
from running away.—Eudora Welty

To freeze-frame a moment is to tether a memory. Like last year when Les and I celebrated our fiftieth wedding anniversary, and afterward our daughter-in-law, Danya, made an album of our celebration. What a cherished gift. One that triggers all sorts of fun emotions. We find a reason every week to pull it out and thumb through it again.

Not all photographs are fun. I came across multiple pictures at a cemetery when my aunt died, when my papaw died, and when my uncle died. Each set of pictures held grief like tears in a hankie. And while it was sad, it's also part of our history. Our story.

My grandmother looks bewildered at the grave site, like she can't figure out how it came to this. Ada was her only daughter, who was in her thirties when she was jilted by her fiancée. Her health failed after that and in a short time she died. Mamaw believed Ada died of a broken heart. I wasn't born yet, so all I have of that day is a picture of my grandmother standing over her daughter's grave.

I have wondered how Naomi survived her losses. The book of Ruth tells us Naomi's losses were multiple. Her husband and both sons died. That's devastating. And even though we don't have photos, we do have Ruth's account. Gratefully, we see redemption in the rest of Naomi's story. I would have loved a photo op of Naomi holding her first "grandchild." I know that baby had to help comfort Naomi and Ruth and heal some of the pain in their hearts.

I have pictures all over my house from my childhood and my husband's. Also pics of our children's childhood and now our grandsons, Justin and Noah. I chose fun pictures of my parents. I have one of my mom as an adult riding a child's tricycle. Very cute. Actually, she was not much bigger than a child with her four-foot-ten stature. And I have one of my dad as an adult lying across his dad's knees as if it he is getting a spanking in front of a woodshed. That makes me smile since my papaw was an unusually quiet man and never lifted his voice, much less his hand. Papaw sipped his coffee out of a saucer and ate his peas balanced on a knife. I wish I had a snapshot of that to show my grandboys.

My favorite photographs are of my grandsons. I have hundreds, but I have refrained from wallpapering our home in them. Instead, I picked out two (for the first floor) that I display regularly and then I have a photo board in our hall that I change out the pictures every month according to a newly established theme. For instance, Noah just had a birthday so it was all about him. For a couple of months it was photos of his childhood, and the next month it was pictures of homes we have lived in. Right now it's a snapshot of two friends, Mary and Luci, who came to visit. It's a way to capture the ever-changing landscape of our lives.

> You don't make a photograph just with a camera. You bring to the act of photography all the pictures you have seen, the books you have read, the music you have heard, the people you have loved.—Ansel Adams

Did you know that with the early cameras of the 1820s, capturing anything on film took several hours? Yikes. So that's why they all looked so grumpy. For a child's photo, the mother had to hold her young children still for hours. The moms were head-draped and disguised as a chair. Isn't that funny? My mother, the chair.

Recently, a man purchased some vintage photographic equipment only to discover negatives inside of it. They turned out to be never-before-seen pictures from World War I. They were taken in France and document some of the destruction of the countryside. That was quite a find.

The most photographed city in the world is . . . New York. Of course the landmark that keeps people snapping their cameras is the Empire State Building. The next most popular city on the top ten list is London. Their famous landmark is Trafalgar Square.

Other popular camera spots in the world are the Eiffel Tower in Paris, Tate Modern in London, Big Ben in London, Notre Dame in Paris, and the London Eye in London.

I have a photo album a friend made of our trip to Africa. It contains wonderful shots of lions we met up close and far too personal. My camera button was almost worn out because there was so much to see that I had never seen before . . . especially set in the wild.

Speaking of wild, I would have thought it momentous if I could have snapped David or Samson with the lions that preyed on them. Now mind you, I wouldn't have wanted to get in the way. I would have liked to be in, say, Nebraska, with a zoom lens.

I guess what I'm trying to say is life is exciting. It's a twirling adventure. Don't miss it! And when possible, capture it. *Snap.*

1. What photographs capture your favorite memories?
2. Do you have an album from a trip to a faraway place (be it Kansas or Calcutta)?
3. Any pictures of wild animals? (My scariest is of my girlfriend's kitten hissing at a stuffed toy in her Michigan living room.)

THIRTEEN
verily

A poem begins as a lump in the throat.

—Robert Frost

I'm excited because in this offering I get to introduce you to a new friend who is teaching me old truths. Nita Andrews is my poetry instructor and my sister in Christ. Nita is also an accomplished artist, which will be obvious to you as she paints pictures even in her writing. She is a woman with rich veins of truth running through her, so don't miss this opportunity to pan her gold. I'm so pleased Nita agreed to write this piece on finding our voice. Get out your pen—you'll want to underline and circle words, lines, and concepts . . . then maybe, just maybe, we, too, will compose, launch our examined life, doodle in the margins, and pen a poem.

Find Your Verily, Verily Voice by Writing Poetry
by Nita Andrews

The Ocoee River in East Tennessee is a wonderful place to go white-water rafting. The river accommodates paddlers on the weekends when water is released from the dam ten miles upstream. At 11:00 a.m. you stand creekside, looking like an insect. There you are, in water shoes and a yellow helmet with a matching yellow, thorax-shaped life preserver. You wonder about your next granola break, and you hold your paddle slack. At 11:15, when the water arrives, it is a different story. The sound of raw power makes you firmly grip your paddle. You stand it upright beside you, you find the belt that weaves around your life preserver, and you tighten it an inch. You forget your vinyl yellow self-consciousness. You even forget granola. You are going to meet this river, and soon!

Every time I have witnessed this transformation I have said to myself, "Life is just like this!" The gift of abundant time arrives new every morning, and it unites with mercy and rushes over me for sixteen hours. I have lots of paddling to do just to keep up, and I have very little time to plot out a course for my approach to the rapids.

In the last year I have tried something different. I have tried to get all the wisdom I can in the hours before the water comes galloping downstream. I have become a student of the riverbed before it is buried under a rolling carpet of whitecaps. I have saved some morning time to watch the lazy river, and it has made all the difference.

One of the ways for me to grow in my faith has been to read and write poetry. I am convinced that the study of poetry has helped me more than anything else to ride the river of hours without drowning in addictions or dark, debilitating moods. Creative writing has helped me build a container for my emotions and the psalms I address to God. One thing that works for me is to have a set-apart time with my pencil when the water is a trickle. I use the time to take stock of my story:

- Have I gone shopping for sport lately?
- Do I avoid something, but I can't think of a logical reason why?
- Have I ever brought more anger to a situation in traffic than the delay or rude driver actually called for?
- Have I sobbed during life insurance commercials on TV? Have I been angry during diamond commercials?

This type of questioning is a good idea. This year I have found that it eased my litany of anxious thoughts to name a pattern and then invite God to show me what has caused a strong reaction on the surface. Any symptom I have can be a guide pointing me to look into what I call the terrain of my riverbed—the terrain of my sorrows. The good news is that deep terrain is best understood in low-water conditions. I look when I am relaxed, sitting on the riverbank, and enjoying the sun like a lizard on a rock. There! In plain sight is an obvious rock. A stumbling place. And what about rushing currents? What about the stubborn ruts of behavior I feel trapped in? There! Look. An eddy! I have seen that rivulets of water during low tide are a miniature version of the flood to come. Good to know.

It is wise to observe where the river will be pushed from one bank to the other, up and over various obstacles. You can ask, "Why does the water wander easily around some shrubs, rocks, and logs, but get snagged on other branches?" I imagine the high tide and see what I will have as landmarks on a future day. And what is going on in the dead spots? What is going on when water sits as still as a car in park? This may be a blue hole of depression that can blindside you.

Can you see how all of these insights hold potential for life change? We learn just as much from the terrain of our greatest joys and our greatest times of union with others or God. Don't forget, they are under the water too. Doing this "examined life" thing in low tide prepares you to grab wisdom with gusto when you find yourself paddling a Class IV rapid—when you don't have time to think.

I read poems on slow days and frenzied days. Life is so hard: it never hurts to seek understanding, and poets can be reliable guides. And what is poetry? It is not your high school English teacher telling you a rhyme scheme. It is not an encrypted puzzle to decipher or a joke with a punch line you will never get. Poetry is a concise way to ask, "What is lurking down there in the depths of me?"

Poets are the deep divers of the heart. They have experience in the darkness. As seasoned divers they can relax further down and breathe in such a way that they get double the amount of air from aluminum tanks the same size as ours. They write of the depths of joy and sorrow. Poets are our first responders. They name the perils attendant to dark corners, unknowns, and deep mysteries. Poets also pull up the treasures of lovely memories. Their gift is to report back to mankind what lies beneath. The great thing about poetry is that even when your eyes look away from the depths, you remain changed by your fresh understanding.

This is the reason that poets are asked to fill the radio airways with poems that inspire the soul of the nation when a crime or catastrophe occurs. This is the reason poets get tapped to read at celebrations. They are uniquely qualified to express gratitude because they are the peculiar ones, like King David. They write psalms and lead corporate worship. The words within poems transcend finite measures like time and fashion. They tell me, "Nita! Wake up! There is more than the clever white water—always more than the rolling surf of easy answers." If I listen to them my kayak may not crack in half when I fall down a flume shaped like the letter *I*. How wonderful to intuit how the currents are shaped, minute by minute, by the riverbed below me.

Poems have helped me imagine heaven and render praise for God's creation, and they have taught me about relationships. Most of all I find the language of the heart inside poems. So I compose. I name. I keep a dream journal, and I scribble down my thoughts in short lines. Some days I doodle in my margins until a couple of important words appear.

When I keep my end of the writing date, I find that writing (even a short haiku) puts me back in line with my story and the big picture of redemption. How uncanny that poets have opened so many of my heart's doors! Surprising, I know. But it is true. If you find you are interested in deep diving, here are some ways to join me:

Try writing a verse poem naming a predictable element of your story in a wild new way. For instance, maybe every August you feel sad. Ask the "thing" to tell you why it reappears in your story every year at this time. I think of titles like, "Dear Blues," "Ode to my Dishwasher," "Dear Procrastination," "Ode to Letters Never Sent," "Dear Scales (or the Twenty-Five Pounds I Lose and Gain Every Winter)," or "Dear Mud Season." I have found that if I ask two or three self-limiting questions within a few minutes, a poem pops out under my pen. Here are some examples:

1 What's the one word that I feel about this?
2. What's the hardest thing about this for me?
3. What do I look forward to or dread most about this?

By asking these questions you discover that you actually do have succinct feelings and you can rely on fewer words to describe your predicament. Some think of it as playful editing. You leave the land of imperial writing that annexes thousands of words per idea and camp out on a small island. This writing uses a chisel liberally. Instead of five chapters you have five lines wearing flip-flops and you are granted one coconut for texture . . . but only one.

Writing poetry is like making a reduction sauce. You simmer the stock until most of it disappears as steam. When you are done you have the strongest flavor. Less volume. More flavor. This process of reducing the clutter and finding your heart is the reason poetry is medicinal. It is the cure for a bad case of confusion. I have seldom written my truth out on a page and not felt clearheaded and ready for the rest of my day.

> There is a moment in each day that Satan cannot find, nor can his watch fiends find it, but the industrious find this moment and it multiplies. And when it once is found, it renovates every moment of the day if rightly placed.—William Blake

History books say that poet William Blake was tormented by doubt. It turns out that the devil he refers to here is actually the devil of his dark thoughts. (Sorry, no red cape and pitchfork here, just a hateful recording inside his brain, stuck on repeat.)

The remarkable legacy of Blake is that in spite of thoughts that drew him into chaos, he nobly fought back. He painted his visions and penned his poems. He won out over his "watch fiends." The good news for us today is that we can be as intentional as William Blake and capture a few "rightly placed" moments every day. Here are five practices that are conducive to leading an examined life:

1. Drinking a cup of tea;
2. Taking a walk off the path at a state park;
3. Having a prayer time;
4. Reading a devotional;
5. and now, the new option of writing poetry!

Will you hold on to the truth that your thoughts are original and you have much to say about your ever-changing riverbed? Will you put on courage and fight to know your voice? Someday soon you will smile when you hear the voice you have known was there all along. It may be hard work to narrow down the propaganda of others until you hear what I call your "Verily, verily"* voice. Do it anyway. You can do it! Perhaps in the future I will read something written or recorded from your verily, verily voice and I will be changed.

Finally, launch your examined life and use poetry if you like. Take time to name hidden rocks. Peer into your depths long enough to understand the power that a buried river rock has over the currents that flow up top.

Verily, verily, I say unto thee . . . write your river of poetry. It's in you, words you long to say, I promise.

1. Have you ever written a poem? When?
2. Who is your favorite poet?
3. Recite a poem from childhood.

---

* *Verily* is a King James usage for the word *truly*. It is used ninety-nine times in the New Testament; see John 8:58 for an example.

FOURTEEN
dance

We should consider every day lost on which we have not danced at least once.

—FRIEDRICH NIETZSCHE

Dance is woven throughout creation. Weeping willows' supple branches waltz atop the river's bend, daffodils spin their yellow petals in summer breezes, waves dip and roll across sandy dance floors, while swallows pirouette in flight. The music is in the wind; the leaves hear it and clap with pleasure. And dance doesn't stop with the wind, trees, flowers, waves, and birds.

I have loved to bend and sway since childhood. I remember as a seven-year-old walking on tiptoes around the house for hours, pretending I was a ballerina. Actually, I was for a while. I started lessons when I was four years old, and by the time I was nine I was passionate about ballet. Saturday mornings sparkled for me because that was the day for my classes. It meant getting up early, walking blocks to the dance studio, and walking home again. I didn't mind. It felt like there were wings on my feet. Those wings were clipped when Mom unexpectedly pulled me out of the classes and then within the year we moved to another town. My dreams of being a ballerina were over.

Fast forward fifty-seven years to the 2011 kickoff Women of Faith conference, where the opening of our event featured for the first time a ballet troupe. I stood backstage and wept as I watched the beauty of their performance. I was surprised by my deep emotional response, but every conference, all twelve events, it would happen again. They would dance and I would cry. I couldn't seem to get past a sadness that accompanied my appreciation for their amazing work. Finally, after examining my feelings, I realized it had been a significant loss for me when years earlier I had to drop out of ballet, a loss I obviously had never grieved.

Who knew dance could go so deep in the heart of a child and nest there as loss? My mom didn't know. For that matter, neither did I. I thought about ballet off and on through the years, but I didn't think about it harboring inside me as hurt. Yet almost sixty years later I still had my ballet slippers wrapped in a child's regret.

Ballet slippers full of dance,
who stole your music?
Who tattered your taffeta dreams?
Poor little ballerina twirling in circles
with no one to catch her.
Pink satin ribbons crisscrossed in years,
White-haired child still on toes,
awaits her recital.

Dance is a beautiful way to tell a story and to worship. In one of the dances the girls in the troupe were attired in long blue satin dresses, and they carried bright red umbrellas that they twirled as they danced. I was mesmerized. In another dance, you watched as one of the ballerinas struggled to find her way through life's hardships and finally looked to Christ. The moment she turned her gaze from the world toward the Savior, you knew it, you felt it, you saw it. It was exquisite, and week after week it left me quietly weeping. (Those tears weren't about my regret but they reminded me of my gain when my life turned toward Jesus.) Their closing number at Women of Faith was one of celebration with tambourines and banners. It was hard not to run and join in. It was joyous. Their presentations were absolute femininity, sheer discipline, and pure praise.

I wonder if that was what it was like when the maidens danced with Miriam as they rejoiced over their safe crossing at the Red

Sea? Leaping, laughter, praise, and tears I'm sure were part of the way they allowed their gratitude full expression.

> Dancing is an art, the floor is my canvas,
> and I am the brush. Whatever I create,
> comes from the heart.—Unknown

While having dinner with friends they told me about an older women (in her seventies) who worked in front of a superstore as a greeter. They said she swayed and danced and even twirled as she welcomed every incoming guest. They said it was so fun seeing her enthusiasm that you wanted to go to the store just to experience her vitality.

I'm sure you've seen the flash mobs on YouTube that take place in malls, train stations, and street settings where suddenly one person starts dancing, and others join in until there are a hundred people, who looked like surprised bystanders, all dancing. It leaves one jubilant. There's just something about that many dancing with such exuberance that feels like victory. Over what? Life's intensity perhaps.

When I was growing up, my dad would suddenly break into a fun version of the Charleston. It made me giggle and lifted my spirits every time. I would beg him to do a few steps when I had girlfriends over but mostly he reserved his antics for mom and me. I think his bib overalls made it even more endearing.

If you are a well-seasoned gal like myself, you remember an exercise fellow by the name of Richard who had big hair and a heart for women with weight issues. And the way he helped was to get them dancing to songs from the fifties. He made it so much fun to exercise. Well, almost fun.

Today the big dance-exercise craze is Zumba. May I just say, "Bring Richard back!" Zumba is like Spanx; it hurts my feelings . . . and a few other things. I know it's got to be a good cardio workout, but c'mon folks, surely shifting that many parts at the same time is guilty of moving violations. The class I attended included girlfriends Mandisa and Melinda Doolittle. They were really good at the South American dance moves while I, try as I might, couldn't get that south of the border. I lasted a total of one class, and most of the time I stared in amazement. I admired the discipline and stamina it took, but give me Chubby Checker and the Twist—or better yet a stroll over Blueberry Hill.

Do you dance? If not, I encourage you to try. It is a great way to get your blood circulating. There's proof reported by the *New England Journal of Medicine* that dancing is the only exercise that offers protection against dementia, which includes Alzheimer's.[1] The National Institute on Aging released findings from a twenty-one-year study of seniors seventy-five years old and older. Dancing frequently offered the greatest risk reduction of any activity studied, cognitive or physical.[2]

That alone should get us out of our chairs and onto the dance floors. My favorite spot to dance is my living room . . . with the shades down because some things are best kept under wraps. I now jiggle where I use to wiggle. It ain't pretty.

Some mornings I bound out of bed eager to pirouette into the world, while other days the molasses in my brain saps my strength, putting my dance on hold. So here I go with one purposeful fling.

I'm casting myself full-fledged into life. Watch out, here comes Patsy in her orthopedic tutu. Join me, it's time to dust off our slippers, sisters (of all ages), and let's jeté.

For your enjoyment check out the artist Edgar Degas's work. Over half of his paintings were of dancers. His ballerinas are lovely. I have one of them as wallpaper on my computer; it never fails to please me.

On with the dance!

1. What part has dance played in your story?
2. What's your favorite dance to watch?
3. What in nature dances for you?

fragrance

Thanks be to God . . . who uses us to spread the aroma of the knowledge of him everywhere.

—2 CORINTHIANS 2:14 NIV

The use of perfume has been traced back thirty-five hundred years. (Yes, that was prior to my birth.) Murals found depicted Egyptian ships sailing off to obtain exotic aromatics. Smelling good has been a longtime project of humanity and we've been willing to pay dearly to get it, even if we had to journey to the far parts of the world. I read about a perfume today that costs $12,721.89 an ounce. Yes, an *ounce*. Turns out the bottle is the biggest factor, while the perfume is a mere $31,000 of the $175,000 price tag. The rest is the packaging of gold, crystal, and five-carat diamonds.[1]

I guess we could always become perfumers and get a discount. Of course that type of schooling will take five to seven years, so we might want to invest in a good bar of soap instead. Just sayin'.

Speaking of extravagant, Christ's fragrance is incomparable. He is the Rose of Sharon and the Lily of the Valley. And the closer we walk with him, the more fragrant we become. Recently I read a poem that stirred my heart about Christ's aroma in Communion. Thank you to Raymond A. Foss for allowing me to use his tender words.

The Fragrance of His Life
Bowing my head, my life
after receiving the bread, the wine
my fingers knitted in prayer
lowering my face, to my hands
the fragrance of his life
washing over me,
in that moment, in that instant
the bread, the wine,
an aroma of his sacrifice
mixing with my tears
falling onto my folded hands
trembling in silent prayer.
—Raymond A. Foss

It's fascinating how aromas years later still transport us back to people and places. It's like our nose has a memory. My grandmother's back porch was ripe with tomatoes that sat on her windowsills like redbirds waiting for a handout. To this day when I am near a seasoned tomato, memories of her cozy up to my heart. Mamaw's bedroom held an old trunk full of her treasures, and when she lifted the lid it emitted a musty essence of yesterday and lavender. That legacy continues in my home because I have her trunk, which now holds my treasures with hers. When I open it, and it releases the past, I can almost feel her purple-veined hand stroke my braided childhood hair.

My mamaw use to put dabs of Vicks behind her ears when she was congested. As a kid I thought that very funny. Not so much anymore. My mamaw lived to be ninety-seven and a half years old, so I say Vicks away. Funny thing, I thought my grandmother was ancient all my life and then finally one day she actually was. (Now it's my turn. Yikes.)

Mamaw had a squeaky voice and mostly smelled like pepper-mint candy. Isn't that a great combination? Especially from a child's perspective. She wore funny shoes and underwear, always carried a hankie, and loved the color red. Sometimes Mamaw smelled like Ivory soap, talcum powder, and Vicks, but mostly she was an undeniable waft of sweet peppermint.

My mom's signature fragrance was Avon's "To a Wild Rose" sachet. I loved when she would lean down to kiss me goodnight because even after she had left the room, her sachet lingered right into my dreams. At Christmastime my dad always bought her per-fume from the drugstore along with a box of chocolate-covered cherries. I was eager for the foreign perfume to be used up so we could get back to her familiar scent. My mom was four foot ten, full of spit and vigor, and died when she was eighty-eight and a half years old.

My best friend Carol's fragrance was just like her kitchen, which was always yummy. Always. Carol was iced cookies and vanilla tea. She was an amazing cook, hostess, and artist. Carol had huge eyes and an even larger heart. She was a hard worker, yet she knew how to sit a good chair. I could tell her anything and everything, and I did. Carol's fragrance was secrets, lilacs, and cinnamon. When she was sixty-four and a half, she died. She was both too old and too young to count half years; but when you are dying, and you know it, you count every precious second.

I often wonder what fragrance my grandsons will associate with me. Hm, I think it will be the smell of popcorn. It's their favorite after-school snack at my house. I'm not a great cook so it won't be iced cookies, and it won't be a rosy sachet or tomatoes like Mamaw's porch. Perhaps they'll remember the waft of magnolia blossoms in the breeze from our front porch swing. Their dinner-plate-size blossoms are extravagant in their offering. Oh, I hope so. I'd love to be associated with something that fragrant, wouldn't you?

To the three women who continue through their fragrant memories to companion me on my journey—my mamaw, my mom, and my dear Carol, who all loved Jesus—I dedicate Arthur Symons's poem, "As a Perfume."

As a Perfume
As a perfume doth remain
In the folds were it has lain,
So the thought of you, remaining

Deeply folded in my brain,
Will not leave me: all things leave me:
You remain.
Other thoughts may come and go
Other moments I may know
That shall waft me, in their going,
As a breath blown to and fro,
Fragrant memories: fragrant memories
Come and go.
Only thoughts of you remain
In my heart where they have lain,
Perfumed thoughts of you, remaining.
A hid sweetness, in my brain.
Others leave me: all things leave me:
you remain.
                                    —Arthur Symons

Today, I have a bowl of peppermint candy at my front door . . . a hankie in my purse . . . and yep, on occasion, a dab of Vicks behind each ear.

1. What fragrances surge with memories for you?
2. What is your personal fragrance?
3. What fragrance comforts you?

SIXTEEN
brave

It is easy to be brave from a safe distance.

—Aesop

Recently I came across a snapshot, in my picture drawer, of a stampeding family of elephants. I took the shot while hanging over the side of a hot-air balloon. What fun! Okay, maybe I wasn't hanging, perhaps I was peeking, but nonetheless I took the picture.

If anyone would have told me I would go to Africa and ride in a hot-air balloon, I would have had you checked for rabies. I don't do heights, and Africa was not on my bucket list because quite honestly it sounded too dangerous. You know lions, hippos, and such.

Besides, it was too far away. Anything over two planes is too much. This trip would require five flights one way, and one of them was the size of a mosquito, flown by a young girl, and landed on a dirt strip. A *dirt strip*, I tell you!

But what started as a resistant spirit inside of me turned into an admission of wonder. I was right that you do have to beware in Africa, but not of the wild beasts. No, it's of losing your heart to this mysterious continent and its resilient people.

Like sentinels, the acacias stand in a sea of endless land that runs into the dusty pink clouds. Herds of zebra as far as the eye can see stripe the dry scape as they make their way toward water. A lone hyena with bony shoulders heckles from a sneering distance. Giraffes sway and nibble on tree tops. And then there are the lions . . . hello.

Oh, Africa, how could I have known you would stay inside of me like a cherished song? It's as if I had known only ballads and someone introduced me to jazz: a thrilling, heart-moving world of sights and sounds beating with the pulse of its people.

Do not think because I made the journey that I was feeling brave. That wasn't the case. I proceeded with knees knocking. Besides, brave isn't a feeling; it's a doing. Every step of the way it was a choice to keep going. I didn't have to go up in the hot-air balloon, but I knew I'd regret it if I didn't. I knew this fear was a chance to trust God.

That morning a small group of us went out before daybreak and watched the balloon being filled with fiery air. Against the dark morning, before our very eyes, the balloon turned into a great puffy dragon. It was spectacular. As the African sun rose up out of the earth, the heavens received our ship and carried us over the breathtaking Masai Mara. We came down in Tanzania, an exciting landing, near herds of water buffaloes and gazelles. The doing of the experience made me stronger.

For me, the trip to Africa stretched me way out of my comfort zone. I wonder if that's how Old Testament Sarah felt when she gave up her home to move far away to a land she did not know. At least I knew where I was going. Sarah's journey is recorded in Genesis. And if you traced her steps you would see that her exquisite beauty put her in a threatening place, that her barren womb made her at times feel hopeless, and that her choice to go ahead of God's plan left her angry and vengeful. Her story gratefully improves, but when we sift through her past we are aware of her bravery mixed in with her humanity.

Isn't that the way it is? The good, the bad, and the ugly. And I'm not talking about Clint Eastwood. I'm talking about how hard life is, how gracious God is, and how faulty we are. But God knows we are trying. He understands our frailty; he made us. And even though God doesn't prevent hardship and heartbreak from touching our stories, he uses the good, the bad, and the ugly to infuse us with courage and compassion.

I'm convinced God doesn't enable us to be brave so we can pat ourselves on the back, but he helps us to be brave to be a light of hope to others who are struggling to find a way. Others' bravery inspires me. Women often whisper their stories to me at conferences, and I am humbled by their courageous attitudes. At times I wonder how they have survived multiple losses, betrayal, financial ruin, slander, terminal illnesses, and so on while retaining their dignity and joy. And yet they carry on, backs straight and determination set. They have been forced to learn bravery and in doing so they have fought off despair and hopelessness. Their candle has turned into a lantern and a beacon compelling others to stay the path and head toward the light.

I met a woman recently who is living in an abandoned warehouse because she is homeless. And while her circumstances seemed dire, her twirling spirit was impressive. She was quick to laugh and to speak of Jesus. She told me when she first slept there she had the lights on, which highlighted the vast space, and she was afraid. She said she prayed and God spoke to her and told her to turn out the lights and that he would be her light. She turned out the lights and to her surprise she went right to sleep. She looked at me and said, "It doesn't matter what size house you live in if Jesus is with you."

I don't know the ins and outs of her story that led her to the warehouse, but I do know her life has not been easy. And because she is different partly as a result of her background, it's hard for her to adjust into social circles. But she hasn't given up trying. I think she's brave. Very brave.

Joseph (in the Old Testament) was different. And boy, did he have social issues . . . even in his own family. He had a truckload of brothers and none of them was fond of his dreamer brother (except for the youngest). Joseph seemed like a troublemaker to his family. And when they sold their misfit sibling into slavery, they were glad to be rid of him. Little did they realize that years later their crazy brother would hold their fate in his hands. Joseph had come up through the ranks of bravery, surviving slavery, false accusations, and prison, and now held the second most influential position in Egypt. Who knew?

Here's to the crazy ones. The misfits. The
rebels. The troublemakers. The round pegs
in the square holes. The ones who see things
differently. They're not fond of rules, and they
have no respect for the status quo. You can
quote them, disagree with them, glorify or
vilify them. About the only thing you can't do
is ignore them. Because they change things.
They push the human race forward. And
while some may see them as the crazy ones,
we see genius. Because the people who are
crazy enough to think they can change the
world, are the ones who do.—Steve Jobs

God uses the peculiar, the odd, the broken . . . in other words, he
uses us. I never imagined that God had such an imaginative plan for
me. I was a rebellious child, a high school dropout, a teenage bride,
and an adult agoraphobic. I couldn't envision good coming out of
the mess I had made. Only God. With a redemptive stir he began
teaching a scaredy-cat to be brave. God's generosity has no limits.

What are you afraid to do? Are you willing to practice bravery
and face that scary obstacle? It helps when we understand that even
if we try and fail we have succeeded at an important developmen-
tal and spiritual level. We learn that we have more chutzpah than
we realized and that Christ meets us as clearly in our failures as
he does our successes. He uses the content of our experiences to
increase our understanding of who he is and therefore who we can
become.

Don't feel brave? Join the throngs of missionaries, martyrs, and Christian mystics. Even if our knees are knocking, we are in good company. Press on.

1. What's the bravest thing you've ever done?
2. How did brave feel?
3. How do you handle the times when you feel different?
4. Do you have a bucket list?

SEVENTEEN

sorrow

*Where you used to be there's a hole in the world, which I
find myself constantly walking around in the daytime, and
falling in at night.*

—EDNA ST. VINCENT MILLAY

Loss is personal—and common. You can't survive this
life without experiencing it.

I remember when I was twelve a tropical fish died in our aquar-
ium. And while it's hard to bond deeply with fish (they are hard
to pet or cuddle), because I was at an age where I was volatile with
fresh hormones, I made quite a scene over that marble-eyed, bloated

golden bundle's demise. Of course, my near hysteria could have been brought on because in an attempt to rescue the floater, I tried pressing on its extended tummy only to have it explode on my hand. Yes, explode. I know, gross. After a dozen sessions of washing and rewashing my hand, I finally placed the fish's ragged remains in my best stationery, tied it with a gold bow, and buried it in the front yard under a bush. My father stood nearby trying to feign grief. The next day I was at the beach playing water tag with my friends.

If only all loss was that easy to recover from.

When I was growing up, we moved frequently. For me, every move was a loss. A giving up of friends, familiarity, school, a sense of stability and safety. But I was a kid and everyone said kids adapted. And I did, but not without a price. There's something to be said for families who live in one home and community all their lives. It doesn't prevent other losses, but it does offer something foundational.

I once had a dog named Hunter. He was my first and only dog while I lived at home. Hunter was an ill-behaved, unruly friend, but he was mine. Until one day I came home from school and he was gone. I've wondered if my parents gave him away because he was disruptive, but I don't know that for sure. They made no attempts to find him that I saw. No posted signs. No newspaper ads. No drives around the neighborhood. There's always a chance he did just run off; he was a scamp. Or he could have been hit and died and my parents wanted to spare me the hurtful news. I think not knowing complicated my loss. I finally stopped scanning the land-scape for him when we moved the following year to another town.

A pet is a significant loss, but it doesn't compare to the death of a person. My first introduction to that kind of heart casualty was when a neighbor's baby died. I had babysat for their young daughter before their baby boy was born. News came from a friend that the neighbor's baby had died from sudden infant death syndrome. I told my mom, and I remember that I felt so awkward saying the words out loud. And then I did something so unexpected . . . I smiled.

To this day it continues to bother me that I did that. I was so unprepared for that profound a loss. I felt confused and embarrassed. Mom didn't seem to notice my inappropriate reaction. She was caught up in the shocking news and our neighbor's crushing loss. She immediately tried to see what she could do for them and seemed unaware that I needed some help understanding my own chaotic heart. I didn't go to the funeral and I don't remember why, but not going left something in me untied.

Our other neighbor's son died at age ten from leukemia. I knew the family well. His sister was a constant playmate, but I didn't attend that funeral either. Maybe it was the way parents protected their children in those days from the harsh reality of death. But I'm not sure which is harder: not knowing or fully knowing.

I would be an adult before I stepped a significant loss all the way through to the cemetery. My husband's seventeen-year-old stepsister, Candy, died in a car accident. It knocked the breath out of us. A few years later my brother was killed in a car accident when he was thirty-eight and I was twenty-seven. A devastating loss for our family. Four years later we buried my dad, who died from cancer. Others would follow.

Within each of us there is a cemetery of sorrow. It is a legitimate place where the losses throughout our lives accumulate and one we must visit repeatedly to do our grief work. Grief is often untidy. We can't wrap our losses in fine stationery and tie it up with a bow. Instead, they come layered in memories, regrets, and unresolved conflicts. So to revisit our cemetery is healthy because grief is often ongoing and done in seasons. Visits are necessary for our well-being, as long as we don't take up residency among the tombs.

I'm often asked how long we should grieve, but grief can't be standardized. Nor can we say how another person should go about it. There is often division in a family when a death occurs because of misunderstandings about each other's grief style.

Some folks after a significant loss get busy. Obsessively busy. They run hard and fast hoping to fall face-first into a sleep that will help them escape the pain that's chasing them. Others sit, sleep, and eat themselves into greater misery or starve themselves into a state of illness. Some take up a crusade to help give the loss a purpose, while others isolate so they don't have to talk about the one who is no longer there. And some become bitter, blame, and refuse to be comforted.

Here's what I've noted . . . everyone is trying to survive their own agony with the skill set they have. We may be sloppy at it, but most of us are doing the best we know how. We must drop our judgment of how someone else is grieving and recognize that even though it's different from our way, it doesn't make them wrong. We tend to hold up our style of how we deal with the ache in our heart as the right way to do it, which means other ways are not acceptable. This is especially true in a marriage when a child dies. We marry an opposite personality, but we seldom are prepared when they grieve in an opposite way than us. A lot of grace needs to be offered during this emotionally crushing blow, over an extended time period . . . like forever.

Verbalizing helps. Not everyone is wired that way. That is where a pastor, counselor, or wise friend may be able to be a mediator. Grieving is a slow process.

As we grieve God uses the hole left in our hearts as a cup to hold compassion for others. If we don't grieve we will seethe, splinter, or go emotionally numb. And if we don't do our grief work (feeling the pain of our losses) we will be unequipped and afraid of other people's pain, lest it set off our own and we not survive it.

> [The Lord] heals the brokenhearted and
> binds up their wounds.—Psalm 147:3

How do we do grief work? Talk about it with someone who knows how to guide you. Write about it. Putting your pain into words that you can see can be helpful. Otherwise we have half-formed thoughts that leave us muddled. If you are running like a house afire, try being still and make peace with the quiet. If you have sunk into lethargy, begin to move toward the light; get out and breathe the fresh air. If you're talking too much, slow down your speech. If you're not talking, find your voice and put your feelings into words. This all takes vulnerability and courage.

Granted, none of this is easy. But we serve a gracious and compassionate Savior, who understands our heartbreak. And while we must grieve he doesn't want us to live in the cemetery. Christ longs to help us expand our zip code that we might reenter life more able to offer grace.

1. What was your earliest loss?
2. What loss ruptured your heart?
3. How did you grieve that loss?

EIGHTEEN
bubbles

There is no angry way to say "bubbles."

—Anonymous

One of the features in my Tennessee home that immediately drew me in was a footed tub. It was so romantic looking with its clawed feet and deep interior. I could imagine myself luxuriating for endless hours in lavender scent with Beethoven's *Moonlight Sonata* bubbling throughout the room.

But quite honestly, mostly, I shower in time to the Big Ben clock ticking in my head and the scent of hurry clinging to my towel. I think showers fit my fast pace, while baths slow me down. So when

I do take the time to soak, I am reminded of a bath's great therapeutic benefits and my great need to deliberately sit a spell.

What is without periods of rest will not endure.—Ovid

Frothy bubbles and gentle music invite me to unwind. And who doesn't need that? I mean, really, in this accelerated, uptight world we are stripping our own gears. Ovid is right: if we don't take time to rest, we deplete our energies. So why do I resist?

I've never been a naturally disciplined person, so it's always taken an all-out effort for me to initiate balance in my zippy approach to life. Yet I find when I do add enhancers like naps, baths, and meditation to my days, I have more to give to others. I'm kinder, saner, and better focused. Not to mention less dizzy from riding that tin horse, Frenzy. And less susceptible to hurt feelings, moods, and inflexibility.

My psychologist friend told me she uses the tub as a boundary. She made a deal with herself to think only good thoughts when she slides into the warm water each night before bed. For her it's a time of letting go of the day's frustrations, inconveniences, and interruptions. She finds bathing the perfect climate for practicing praise.

Do you have a favorite soap? A fluffy towel? Some relaxing music? That's all it takes . . . oh yes, and some time. That may be the hardest thing to extract from your day, but you might be enticed to try harder when you realize all the ways you win if you do.

When we glow (sweat), it removes toxins from our bodies. The hot bath kills many strains of bacteria and increases our blood flow;

our blood flow repairs damaged tissues. And I'm told it improves our immune systems, helping us avoid and recover from colds and infections. Drop in a little olive oil and it will help rid us of that dead skin on our feet, legs, and elbows.

We must always change, renew, rejuvenate
ourselves; otherwise we harden.
—Johann Wolfgang von Goethe

Johann isn't referring to just the calluses on our feet, but the ones that can form on our attitudes and heart when we thin out our reserves.

Years ago I stopped to visit a friend I hadn't seen in a long time and realized she was in trouble. Her once-resilient mind now trailed, her sharp focus was splintered, and the bright flicker in her eyes was flat. After a long conversation I realized the trying situation she was in had used up her reserves and she was headed toward a breakdown if something didn't change soon. Even the simplest decision had become too much for her to handle emotionally.

I contacted her family in another state and expressed my concerns, and they immediately intervened. For a season she did nothing but rest and take long baths until she slowly recovered. All decision making was taken off her plate until she was renewed in her mind. Eventually she became the vibrant gal we all had known her to be.

It can happen to anyone. I know. It was about twenty years ago when I pushed too long and too hard and toppled into a pit of depression. My counselor called in my husband and instructed him to clear my calendar for three months. I had forgotten, from my agoraphobic days, how much depression weighs. For those three months I rested and allowed my body a chance to recalibrate. I paid attention to my diet, I journaled for my emotions, and yes, I took baths in the evening. It helped take the edge off my tension. At the end of my time off I felt like a new person. My head was clear, my body was recharged, and my emotions were in a much better place.

We need to have boundaries in this invasive world that allow us a time and place to refuge and recover. And we need to be aware of our limitations. Nobody was designed to twirl all the time.

LeeLee, my nine-year-old next-door neighbor, appeared on my front porch a few days ago with a warm smile and a cellophane-wrapped gift in her outstretched hand. It was a handmade bar of lavender soap that she and her grandma had whipped up. I was delighted that they would think of me in such a sweet way. After she left, as I held the soap, I wondered if it was time to reinstate baths into my rushed routine. I needed a spa-like experience.

Spas are big business today, and there's not one worth its weight in candle wax that doesn't offer some type of bathing experience for its therapeutic value. We can bring that type of therapy right into our homes at little expense by adding a few drops of essential oils, salts, herbs, and flowers into our bath waters. Scent makes our bathing experience so inviting and relaxing.

I'm told if you use lavender oil it will help you relax, whereas sweet orange or grapefruit oil will be invigorating. To energize, spearmint and rosemary oil are supposed to be a good blend. Careful, don't energize too late or you could be up all night cleaning chimneys and replacing roof tiles. Also, if you have high blood pressure, if you're pregnant, or have other ailments, avoid essential oils without your doctor's approval. I am allergic to certain fragrances, so I am particularly cautious.

> Noble deeds and hot baths are the best
> cures for depression.—Dodie Smith

(It might not be quite that simple, Dodie, but it's a great beginning.)

Let's make good choices, pace ourselves, listen to our bodies, establish healthy boundaries, and soak up a fresh outlook.

1. What are your favorite bath products?
2. Do you have a Big Ben clock ticking in your head? How might you soften its impact?
3. When is the last time you gave your body permission to recalibrate?

NINETEEN

evergreen

> *A nation that destroys its soils destroys itself. Forests are the lungs of our land, purifying the air and giving fresh strength to our people.*
>
> —Franklin D. Roosevelt

I love evergreens. I even love their name. And since moving to the South I have a new second favorite, the magnolia. It just happens my neighbor has a beautiful magnolia tree in her front yard. I'm surprised she hasn't cited me for invasion of privacy since I keep sticking my nose in her tree. I can't help it; I'm smitten. Truly.

The Southern magnolia, when given the space and light it needs, can grow over two stories high; but it also can grow to be no larger than a bush. It's adaptable to its environment. By its nature it draws songbirds into its branches. Isn't that smart? It's an outdoor concert hall. Its flowers are the size of dinner plates and the leaves are waxy green with a bronze underside. The blossoms are parchment in color and are divinely fragrant. They are real showstoppers. They are a member of the evergreen species, so they continue to look full and inviting all year.

I want to be like a magnolia tree. I want to be adaptable, I want to keep a song tucked close to my center, I want to be fragrant, and I want to be ever-green. My life verse is to be "like a tree" (Psalm 1:3).

When we bought our Tennessee home it had a seventy-foot tree in the middle of the driveway. Yep, the middle, which left us squeezing between the house and the tree to get to the garage. Oh, did I mention we share the driveway with our neighbors? This made it even more interesting with the neighbors and us skirting the tree at the same time. I'm sure we looked like a wacky version of dodge 'em cars.

One day my hubby, Les, was talking to a man who owned a lawn service and the man mentioned to Les that the tree was a danger to our home because it wasn't healthy. Hm. It looked healthy to me, so I ignored the warning. A year went by and our son, his wife, and our grandchildren moved in with us for a season. Their bedrooms were upstairs by the tree. Now that changed the equation, because I couldn't leave something up that was a possible danger to them. What kind of nana would I be? My mom taught me to love trees, but not more than people, so I hired a company to take it down.

The day the service arrived I was relieved and sad. It took two days and a couple of trucks to haul it away. About halfway through the cutting down process, we discovered the tree had no middle. It had literally rotted away. There was at least thirty-five feet of rottenness, and it was growing its own mushroom colony inside.

The following week a tornado swept through our town, flipping cars and taking down many large trees. Even though that doesn't mean ours would have fallen, it felt reassuring to have it down safely. I was reminded yet again to listen to those who are trained and know the danger signs. Also, you can't always judge a tree by its bark (much like people).

Last summer the state sent trimmers out to tidy up the trees lining our downtown streets (which by law are legally theirs), but I was not prepared for what happened to the beautiful maple in front of our home. I took precautions, like being there when they arrived. I pointed out how it needed a gentle trim to maintain its almost perfect shape. I offered all the workers cold water and sodas and showered them all in smiles. At first as they cut into the tree's limbs I thought it looked aggressive, but I knew after our friendly conversations they wouldn't do any unnecessary cutting. So I tried to trust them and not look. I chatted with a friend on my porch when suddenly a neighbor ran out, hands flailing, and yelled to me, "Can't you stop them? They are ruining your tree." I turned around and was dismayed. They had chopped away at the maple beauty like they needed a woodpile for the winter. And they had no intentions of stopping.

"Stop!" I heard myself scream. Oh yes, it was a scream, because I had to be heard above the equipment, and trust me I was. Suddenly the saws stopped and all the workers turned and stared at me. "No more!" I stated emphatically. They made a call to their supervisor, who came right over to survey the matter (and the wild woman). When he got there and saw my poor hacked-up tree, he became quiet. He and his men had a private chat, then they packed up and left. The damage was done. The tree was an embarrassing wad of hacked-up limbs on the top and out of the middle, while the lower outside remained long and now creepy and spider-like.

I've almost recovered. It's been four months. I've finally stopped looking at the straggly tree and cringing every time I go in and out of the house. Our friends across the street have a large maple as well. Before the "trim," our trees met in the middle of the street, forming a glorious canopy of fall color that people came from all over to applaud. But no more. I was told recently by the man who warned us about our driveway tree that our maple would now begin to die and limbs would be endanger of falling. The following week the first limb came colliding down landing in the street. It's so sad.

Did I mention I love trees?

I believe in tree planting for the environment's sake as well as for beauty's sake. Trees offer oxygen, shelter, shade, storm drainage, air pollution control, and fruit. After my mom's passing I received a gift of a tree to commemorate her life. I loved that gift and she would have too. I chose a Bartlett pear with my gift certificate. The pear tree flowers in spring like a girl's ruffled skirt and it becomes handsomely bronze in the fall. It is a tree full of sass and beauty and represents Mom well.

A tree says: My strength is trust. I know
nothing about my fathers, I know nothing

about the thousand children that every
year spring out of me. I live out the
secret of my seed to the very end, and I
care for nothing else. I trust that God is
in me. I trust that my labor is holy. Out
of this trust I live.—Hermann Hesse

The Scripture mentions trees from the first verses in Genesis right up to the closing chapters in Revelation. The Lord appeared to Abraham by the terebinth trees of Mamre. We are told that Deborah sat under a tree to dispense wisdom. Elijah slept under a broom tree and was awakened by an angel. Zacchaeus shimmied up a tree and went out on a limb to catch a glimpse of Jesus. Most important, Jesus hung on a tree for our sins. And there will come a day when the trees shall sing for joy and their leaves will be used for the healing of the nations.

Recently, hundreds of migrating robins landed in our yard. The trees were full of song, but I have to admit they were not well orchestrated. It was more a cacophony than a symphony. One day, though, the birds will be in perfect pitch and the trees and even rocks will join them in shouts of praise. Singing trees, now that will be something.

1. What is your favorite tree?
2. Would you consider planting a tree on your property this year? If so, what kind?
3. What quality of a magnolia tree would you like to see grow in your life?

TWENTY

sparrow

For a lack of attention, a thousand forms of loveliness elude us every day.

—EVELYN UNDERHILL

Birds rule.

Okay, maybe they don't rule, but they rock . . . at least they do in my world. Show me a flock of birds flying in formation and you have my full attention. Call me to a window to witness a bird I've never seen before and you will be on my best friend forever list. Or let me sit on your porch in the earshot of a sparrow's song, and I'll serve you iced tea by the buckets full.

I'm not sure when this bird stuff first pecked at my heart, but I think it was when we moved to the Boy Scout Reservation (true). That's when my first feeders went up. They were right outside my kitchen window, and because we lived in the woods they were a hot spot for many feathered friends. And as the seasons changed in Michigan so did the population and colors at my feeders. By winter, with the snow piled high on the evergreen limbs, the cardinals' flash of red and the blue jays' dapper suits of blue captured my artistic fervor . . . forever smitten.

My husband's mother's maiden name was Cardinal. Isn't that lovely? My maiden name was McEuen. Harder to give it wings. McEuen lends itself more to kilts while Cardinal conjures up aviaries and slashes of red flight across the path of the morning sun.

I wonder if the young blue heron was shopping for an aviary or was blinded by the sun when he landed in our yard a few years ago. Once he landed it seems he couldn't figure out what to do and was running around in frenzied circles. I wasn't home for his initial arrival, but my husband was. Being a tenderhearted, hospitable man, he captured the tall, skinny, befuddled creature and put him in a large cage in our garage. To give you an idea of this bird's height, he and I were eye to eye, and I'm a whopping five foot nothing. How do I know we were the same height? That happened when I opened the garage door and to both of our dismay, we were staring deeply into each other's eyes.

Wait, let me back up in this story for a minute. When I returned from shopping, my husband smiled as I came through the door and said, "Go look in the garage. There's a surprise." Intrigued, I headed back out the door and made my way around to the garage.

I love surprises. I speculated maybe a new car (ha), a candy-red motor scooter, or a flashy ten-speed.

And I must say in his defense that my husband had no idea the bird was loose when he sent me out there, because he had securely (ha) caged him. That is how I knew the heron was skinny because he had literally wiggled his way between the bars of the cage to escape. And I know that because when big bird looked into my baby blues, he turned around, ran back to the cage, and wiggled his way back in. (Kind of hurt my feelings.)

I screamed and ran for the house (which probably hurt his feelings).

All that clamor was not the reaction Les had expected to his fun "surprise," as I raced past him screeching. Later, once my palpitations stopped, my screech turned to laughter. Today when I relive that chance meeting in my head, it gets funnier and funnier. Too bad there wasn't a video cam going to catch our nose-to-beak encounter, the bird's hasty retreat to self-imprisonment, and my mad dash. It would have been a YouTube sensation, I'm sure.

As much as I like viewing birds, I don't want to house them, have tea with them, or buff their beaks. I just want to observe their beauty from a respectable distance and soak up their songs. (To ease your mind, later that day a wildlife warden picked up the wayward bird that he said had left the nest too young, before his GPS had kicked in. And he was going to care for him until he matured. Les decided to keep me, too, hoping for the same results.)

Unlike me, Old Testament Elijah wanted up-close exchanges with birds, since God had assigned them to feed his prophet. And when you have no source of food and a raven shows up with sushi your gratitude level tends to soar.

Birds are frequently mentioned in Scripture, from being bearers of good news, to being dinner, to being reminders of God's care for us. We are compared to a sparrow—a small, average-looking bird with a playlist of songs that cause maestros to weep.

People weep when I sing as well, but for an altogether different reason. It has been so humbling during my speaking career to sing in the vicinity of songbirds Sandi Patty, Kathy Troccoli, Nichole Nordeman, Nicole C. Mullen, and Mandisa, just to name a few. My singing not only hurts ears; it hurts people's feelings. I keep hoping to one day open my beak, I mean, mouth, and sound like a female version of Andrea Bocelli.

Even though we won't all be able to twirl our voices like Natalie Grant here on earth, we can have a song of Christ in our hearts during our journey, one that adds a melody to our lives everywhere we go. As a child I remember my mom singing the lines from an old hymn, "There's within my heart a melody, Jesus whispers sweet and low . . ." Her voice, while only a squeak better than mine, was beautiful when she sang about the Savior. It was calming and reassuring for this little sparrow to hear her mom sing of his love.

Did you know sparrows have a bone in their tongue to help them break apart seeds? Honest. Isn't that odd? But oh so provisional. God knew what he was doing. His execution of design was stellar. Now if we can hold onto that thought for ourselves. God has made no mistake with us. When we were knit together it was done well: he provided for our need before we even recognized what to ask for, and he created a space inside our hearts for not just any song but a new song. One that will harmonize our existence and sing of his.

"He has put a new song in my mouth. Praise to our God." (Psalm 40:3).

1. What is your favorite bird?
2. When was the last time you wanted to fly away?
3. What does the song in your heart sound like?

TWENTY-ONE
be

If there's no peace in our pace, we're not in Christ's race; we are running one of our own.

—PATSY CLAIRMONT

I confess: I'm a Twitter gal, a Facebook friend, a Pinterest pal, an Instagram follower, and a disjointed blogger. Yes, I need therapy. And quite honestly, I can't think of a better therapist than our Wonderful Counselor, Jesus. His office is located next to still waters and quiet resting places.

Uh-oh, Geronimo, this could be a problem. Quiet? Rest?

Those of us who are tied tight, who run hard and do much, tend to have trouble believing "stillness" is sacred work. We value tangible results. We are into sweat equity. We believe if we are working you should be too—that is, if you are worth your weight in coffee beans, which we consume by the vat. And certainly we prove our belief in busy by our extensive to-do lists and our relentless productivity. Just check the thinning treads on my Nikes.

The problem isn't in what we achieve, but at what cost. We are now a nation of sleep-deprived folks who are overmedicated and anxiety ridden. We have a dismal record of divorces, so obviously things are tense on the home front. Too many children are cutting themselves, purging, and gaining access to weapons. And our entertainment is filled with pornography and violence.

I would think our society's symptoms are reason enough for us to consider change. Do I believe sitting quietly is going to change our world? I think sitting quietly before the Lord is an honorable and necessary beginning . . . for us, for our nation, for the world.

"Be still, and know that I am God" (Psalm 46:10). This has to be one of the most widely distributed scriptural reminders in print today. So why isn't it helping? Perhaps we are drawn to this verse because it tucks inside a tweet, frames easily for a wall hanging, and isn't hard to memorize. But for our social media mentality, it's hard to embrace in practicality. I mean, where do we fit the practice of "still" into our race to the finish line?

The above verse begins with "be." Not "do." *Be* is a breathe word. *Be* is an invitation in and of itself to surrender. Just be. Not run. Or fret. Or even produce. Be present. Be quiet. Be aware. Be ourself. Be Christ's.

The word *be* is worth our quiet consideration. Maybe we could better assimilate it if we made it a meditative prayer. "Oh, Lord, as I sit in your presence, teach me to be."

"Still" gives direction to our "be." *Still* is an action word that requires us to quietly reposition our energies. *Still* appears in direct opposition to our expressway lifestyle, but actually the *still* helps give our *do* its purpose. When I linger in the quiet, it feels like the commotion inside me takes a coffee break long enough for me to feel more tethered to Christ's purposes. Running at full throttle I can dash past important moments only to look back later and regret that I didn't take time to pat a back, kiss a forehead, or say a kind word. I seem to be more present when I have stilled my heart in quietness and when I have asked the Lord to guide my hours and moderate my hyper tendencies.

"And know" invites us to engage our brains in the meditative process. It's not a holy nap time; it's a holy cap time. A time when we put on our thinking caps and consider who or what rules our lives. Is it our boss, our obligations, peer pressure, our goals, our drive? Settling the matter of who is ultimately in charge of us is huge, because it takes so much frantic pressure off us. *Knowing* is a kneeling word. One that reminds us to acknowledge God's sovereign care over us. I don't have to bear up; I just need to kneel down so I can rise up confident in his lordship.

"He is God." Not he *was* God, or he *is going to be*, but he *is*. *Is* is past, current, and future. *Is* doesn't have a limited warranty clause with it. *Is* takes us throughout our lifetime and all future generations. *Is* doesn't waver. And "He is God" designates his position and power. At the name of God, wise men kneel and kings fall prostrate. We would do well to do likewise.

Here are a few practical steps I've taken to open up spaces for stillness to permeate my ricochet schedule.

- I've cut back on my Internet time.
- I dropped out of two classes I was attending.
- I cut back on TV viewing. I am now down to three shows.
- I put boundaries around my painting time.

Are there any places you might edit in your busy spaces to make room for God to press "be still" inside of you?

Don't misunderstand, I believe in a work plan and staying in touch with technology . . . just not marrying it, which isn't easy to avoid if you're a techno-junkie. I love gadgets, as do the men in my life and most of my friends. So this will be a toughie. I'll have to discipline myself when the next slick new work toy is released. Ouch.

I also love results I can see. But God is teaching me that his most important work is done where we can't see. He excavates the heart.

Let's not waste the gift we've been given of time and life. Running too fast jeopardizes the quality of our interior and the impact of our exterior offerings. Keep short accounts with the Lord; he's available to guide us all the way home. He will teach us in the stillness the value of our moments.

We have only this moment, sparkling
like a star in our hand—and melting like
a snowflake.—Marie Beynon Ray

Life is sacred . . . twirl out of sheer gratitude!

1. Are you more of a *be* person or a *do* person? Explain.
2. How does the silence make you feel?
3. How has God taken care of you?

cuddle

*Such short little lives our pets have to spend with us, and
they spend most of it waiting for us to come home each day.
It is amazing how much love and laughter they bring into
our lives and even how much closer we become with each
other because of them.*

—JOHN GROGAN

Davidson sent me flowers.

Davidson is a feline.

A big, yellow, striped cat.

We bought our home from a lovely couple who moved across

town. In a turn of events Davidson's owners ended up buying and moving into another home back on our street, one house away. But nobody could convince Davidson that he didn't still live at our house. So when he came calling the first time at our back door crying to get in, we didn't know where he came from.

One day we left our garage door open and Davidson dashed in, ran up our steps, and hid. From what we could surmise he had been up there two days before we spotted him in the attic window and rescued him. Davidson must have enjoyed the adventure because it became a game. He snuck in every chance he got, hid, and then his owners would come looking for him.

Poor Davidson. His homing devices hadn't caught up with his homes. Finally, we deterred Davidson from becoming an innocent victim of our box-strewn attic by installing a children's gate at the foot of the steps. This has worked so far, but I see him patrolling the grounds trying to figure out why he isn't allowed to luxuriate in the pools of warm sun in one of his favorite old haunts.

Now back to the flowers. My doorbell rang one evening, and when I answered it there stood Davidson's owners with a red vase of flowers. Extending the vase, they said it was Davidson's way of saying thank you for our hospitality.

Aw, Davidson, sweet.

Truth be known, I have a penchant for dogs, but then I grew up watching Lassie, Rin Tin Tin, and Bullet. However, Davidson won me over with his passion for home. Besides, who can resist a feline who sends flowers? Also, I've lived in a lot of houses, and some of them I still miss. Given the chance, if no one was looking I would sneak in and prowl around one more time, just to see how the place had fared and how it made me feel to be back in its sunshine. Yes, I get Davidson's need to meander around in the past.

I've always believed in owning pets, from a bird in a cage to a tadpole in a bowl. I think pets bring a sense of companionship. Although I think it's hard to be comforted by a goldfish or smooched by a turtle, so my pet of choice tends to be a fluffy, bouncing, nuzzling dog. One that licks the patent off your leather shoes in his enthusiasm to welcome you.

You've probably read the health benefits of having a pet, which should make all of us rush to the pound. They keep us active, social, playful, and calm. It's been proven that our blood pressure and cholesterol levels drop when we interact with animals. And therapists use dogs to help anxiety-ridden patients deal with their stress. Even prisons have set in place programs using their prisoners to train dogs. These programs have helped to lower violence among inmates and provide a service for communities. So pet interaction has multiple benefits, which are clearly seen in the life-saving heroism of pets and their owners. I found several accounts of dogs who even earned military status for their bravery, one as a sergeant and one as a lieutenant colonel.

For several years at Women of Faith, one attendee brought her small dog inside a pouch on her sweatshirt to warn her if she was going to have a seizure. The dog could detect an oncoming spell before it affected her and would alert her so she could lie down until it passed. Isn't that fascinating?

I read one account about a parrot that started squawking and screeching over and over, "Momma-baby!" "Momma-baby!" (Two of the words from its trained repertoire.) So the mom went into the baby's room and found he was choking and turning blue. She was able to save his life.

A parrot? Wow!

Then there's the cat I read about who got in his sleeping owner's face, crying loudly until the drowsy owner woke up and discovered both her husband and son were already unconscious from a gas leak in the home. She called for help and all were rescued.

A cat? Who knew?

Another feline was honored by the Red Cross for saving the lives of his owners when he awakened them by scratching his owner awake when their house was on fire.

Now there is even evidence that Alzheimer's patients have fewer outbursts if there is an animal in the house. Socially inept children are drawn out of their isolation by pets. Dogs have been known to rescue drowning children, people from snakes and bears, and families from home invasion.

There are approximately 78.2 million owned dogs in the United States and 86.4 million owned cats.[1] That's a lot of kitty litter and doggy treats. But when you understand what they do for us, it isn't too surprising.

The most popular dog breed according to most statistics is the Labrador retriever, and the most popular cats are the Persian and the Siamese. We have had myriad pets through the years—from gerbils, to turtles, to birds, tropical fish, kittens, and puppies. The breeds have been diverse: beagle, Russian wolfhound, poodle, shih tzu, cockapoo, and an assortment of ragamuffin mutts. We loved them all.

My little dog—a heartbeat at
my feet.—Edith Wharton

Regardless of your pet preference, I'm convinced God made these animals for a purpose. It is no mistake that they purr on our laps, nestle near our feet, vie for our attention, and wait eagerly for our arrival.

Need a friend? Need comfort? Need a secret keeper? I mean, honestly, who else is that happy every time, I mean *every time*, you walk through the door? And who knows, one day they may even send you flowers.

1. What pets have you owned?
2. What was your favorite pet? Why?
3. Has a pet ever saved your life? How?

TWENTY-THREE

verve

The words of scholars are like well-driven nails.

—ECCLESIASTES 12:11

If someone told you they could help you get a better job, a promotion, better grades in school, command more respect, make more money, feel more confident, improve your communication skills, and comprehend more, would you be interested?

I would and I am.

Even though I'm coming to the end of the work cycle in my life, I still want to know and to grow. It takes both to benefit (mature). First to learn (know) and then to apply (grow). And one of the ways for us to experience the above list is to improve and expand our vocabulary. I know that sounds too easy. But knowledge of words unlocks meaning, and meaning makes us privy to a world of information, and information offers us options. I personally adore options.

So guess what? We have circled back to the benefits of reading.

Reading improves vocabulary. No doubt about it. Seeing words placed in their rightful surroundings helps us achieve fine grammar. Do you remember memorizing spelling lists in elementary school? If you were like me, you'd memorize them usually the night before the test, squeak through the exam, and a week later you would have forgotten half the list. Today they require children to spell and place the word correctly in a sentence. That's much more effective.

I have found that I can read a word I don't know, but when it's accompanied by other words I do know, they become clues to the mysterious word's identity. Of course, to appreciate the fullness of its offering, we need to be on a best-friend basis with a dictionary. I'm passionate about dictionaries. Especially those wise enough to include sketches or photographs in their design and definitions, since I tend to be a visual learner. (Do you know what kind of learner you are? This will help you by leaps and bounds. Some learn more quickly through the eye-gate, others through the ear. Some are distracted by visuals; others need them.)

One Christmas when I was a child I received, to my initial dismay, a set of encyclopedias that included a huge two-volume dictionary. I could hardly lift them. I surprisingly spent untold hours sitting on the floor, searching through the pages and pictures. In the back of the second book, there was a guide to foreign languages.

I was smitten with curiosity. It was like a world of new friends had entered my life, and to this day dictionaries are some of my favorite tomes. You know the question everyone is eventually asked in their lifetime: "If you were stranded on a desert island and could only have three books what would you take?" Well, the dictionary is my second choice.

My current favorite dictionary is the *American Dictionary of the English Language*. It is a facsimile of Noah Webster's 1828 edition. I have a hard copy, which I enjoy, but you can download this treasure as well. It goes to the root of a word and gives a little history, which I find helpful and often fascinating. But no pictures.

Adding to our vocabulary takes effort, so be prepared to jot down words you hear or see that you are unsure of so you can investigate them. My friend Luci was visiting, and I introduced her to a musical instrument she had never heard of or seen before, the Chapman Stick. She immediately recorded the name and later looked it up online to see what she could teach herself about it. Luci is eighty years old. Investigating people, places, and meanings has been a way of life for her. It shows in the versatility of her communication style. I applaud her ongoing inquisitiveness and mental vigor, which I'm convinced go hand in hand.

We can survive life without an ongoing educational plan, but who just wants to wiggle through, when we can thrive? To a great deal, our known dialogue (what we've grown used to hearing ourselves say) predicts the direction and outcome of our story. Read that line again. Our words have that kind of impact, so it's worth our time and effort to keep our vocabularies lush and lively.

Besides being a dedicated reader, a careful listener, and a list keeper, it helps to be a game player. I personally love Words with Friends, Scrabble, and crosswords. There are tons of word games available, so you can find one that keeps you mentally challenged and verbally crisp.

Occasionally I get a fixation on a word and it pops up so frequently in conversations that it sounds like I have the hiccups. I often hear the stuck record in others' speech as well; it's hard to miss. A common word that's lost its social glitter is *amazing*. If you're verbally addicted to *amazing*, try the myriad other choices you have available. Because after the first five times you say "amazing," people tend to tune out your assessment. Try *impressive, stunning, moving, dazzling,* or *astonishing*. We have choices . . . like ice cream. The same is true for the much-abused *awesome*. Repeated use takes some of the awe out.

Also the word *nice*. It is beige and threadbare. Pleasant is a, uh, nice alternative. Also *courteous, gracious, polite,* or *kind*. And it isn't just the common words that become tiresome with repetition, but any word that keeps ricocheting around in an exchange that can make us crazy. Like *you know*. Word variety heightens other people's interest in what we are saying. And it is a human need to feel heard, so everyone benefits when we communicate well.

See if you know these gems: *Rapacious? Erudite? Suss? Acrimonious?* You might want to explore some fresh choices to enhance your interaction with others and to challenge your intellect. But I'm not suggesting that we become so heady with our choices that no one understands a word we are saying. Instead, let's be continual learners with a twirling vocabulary that is captivating and uplifting.

Every day we should hear at least one little
song, read one good poem, see one exquisite
picture, and, if possible, speak a few sensible
words.—Joahann Wolfgang von Goethe

Enunciation is important if you want to make a smart impression. It's so easy to have lazy language infiltrate our speech. We say "wanna" instead of "want to," and "gotta" instead of "got to"—also the notorious double negatives when we say "can't hardly" instead of "can hardly." These are easy things to clean up if we are paying attention and if we care.

Jesus zeroed in on our intentions under our words when he said, "Let your 'Yes' be 'Yes' and your 'No,' 'No'" (Matthew 5:37).

"Say what you mean and mean what you say" will always hold true. Choosing words that creatively and accurately express our heart and our faith is a gift to others. It's a way to nail down what we believe and why . . . our legacy to a world who awaits our voice. Choose to chime in wisely.

1. How would you note your vocabulary on a scale of 1 to 5 (5 being the best)?
2. How often do you use a dictionary?
3. Do you have any "hiccup" words?

TEWNTY-FOUR
stars

I once had a speedy bicycle that I believed, at night, could
fly me to the heavens and let me touch the glittering hem of
a star.

—PATSY CLAIRMONT

When my boys were young, there was a song we sang together that encouraged children not to spend all their time looking down, kicking cans, lest they miss important things like rainbows and shooting stars passing by. Since my favorite childhood song is "Somewhere Over the Rainbow," and I am an avid fan of star-flung night skies, looking up holds great appeal.

But even with my draw to the heavens it took a long time, after a bleak season, before my spirit looked up. I was a "can kicker" from way back. Remember the neighborhood game of kick the can? Well, I dragged it into my adult life. Depression held such a grip on me that when I started pulling out of it, one day I laughed out loud, and the sound startled me. It was a noise that had burrowed so deep into my cave of despondency that I actually forgot I could laugh.

Here's the odd thing: during those sad years of sloughing thru the thick molasses of moods and misery, I didn't realize I was depressed. You'd think you'd know when you sleep all the time, you don't want to leave home, and you've lost interest in vital activities. But honestly, I didn't get the depth of my sadness until I took important steps into the light. Sometimes contrast and hindsight are the clearest definers.

I wish someone would have told me I was depressed and even more that there was a way out. I might not have believed them and I might have been unwilling to pay the price to get to higher ground . . . I guess I'll never know. I sure wasted a lot of years, although I do believe God is a redeemer and therefore he uses our losses for the gain of his kingdom and the building of our character.

So just in case you are depressed and don't recognize it because it is so insidious, let me remind you. Allow me to hold up a clear sign so you don't waste years wondering what's wrong with you. Naming our challenge gives us an advantage to then plan an escape route.

Our enemy is defined in Scripture as a thief and a liar who comes to steal and destroy. And no, he is not always obvious. He doesn't show up dressed in a red suit poking at us with a pitchfork.

Instead, he comes as a foreboding thought, an accusation, a painful memory . . . as discontent, as fear, and as heaviness. He strews cans in our path and then taunts us to kick them. He realizes if we stay weighted down long enough, our brain and emotions will fog up on us and we'll forget that "up" is a directional choice.

I remember my body feeling too heavy to lift up out of the bed. It seemed I used all my energies in those years to move from chair to bed and back again. Eventually it became easier to just stay in bed. Sad is like saddlebags full of rocks. And even though there are medications that can help to balance out our brain's chemicals and our emotions, we still have to unpack our own saddlebags. But not alone.

One of the big, fat lies of the enemy is we are the only ones suffering like we do and no one understands the depth of our pain. He is a liar, liar, liar. He wants us to feel isolated and alone because that's the zip code where despair breeds.

Despair: to be without hope.
Hope: believing that things will
turn out for the best.

To find hope's uplifting assurance and assistance, I had to make choices that flew in the face of my feelings and fears. My emotions were so contaminated with hopelessness that even my mind was bulging with corrupt files that had to be replaced. That takes time and effort.

Recently, my friend Steve brought me the neatest stack of business-size cards with words of affirmation and hope. They are designed to give out to people you want to encourage or thank. They are simple, done in large print, and their words are positive. These are the type of replacement thoughts I could have used to help in my get-well therapy. Statements like "You are generous," "You are remarkable," and "You are kind." You see, my head told me I was worthless, I was dumb, and I was ugly. What an unfortunate and unhealthy way to live, under the tyranny of the enemy's propaganda.

Not only were my emotions in constant turmoil, but my mental health was affected, or should I say infected. To begin a new path I had to stop kicking the can and purpose to look up and see the stars again. When I learned my will was stronger than my emotions and I could command my body to obey and my mind to think differently, even when I didn't feel like it, that was huge. I repeat, *huge*. But I had to practice it again and again and again. Day after day. I found no shortcut. This was by far the hardest work I had ever done.

What strengthened my resolve was the renewing of my mind. Refusing the lies and replacing them with the truth. Like trading "You are alone" to "Jesus will never leave me nor forsake me." Or refusing the thought "You are hopeless" and replacing it with "Jesus is my hope, and his plans include a future for me." And exchanging the lie "You are worthless" with "You are dearly loved."

The process was strenuous, but the results were definite. I began slowly to think more rationally and live more sanely. I developed mental flexibility and emotional stability.

Here are some signs of depression:

Unrelenting sadness. My loss of positive emotions left so gradually I didn't realize their departure until I felt overcome by sadness.

If I had a theme word during those years, it would have been *over-whelmed*. I was living the life of a victim.

Guilt. Guilt and I were on a first-name basis. I'm unsure what the guilt was about, but we regularly hung out together. Like buddies, I gave her time. I didn't realize how she muddled my value and undermined my faith. I needed to upgrade my friends.

Crankiness. Sad and guilty makes one cranky. Trust me, if you are dealing with a cranky person, it is not about you. Cranky is an inside number. Crankiness comes from the other person's stuff, so don't try to own it for them. It only complicates recovery for both of you.

Fatigue. I slept ridiculously long hours and never felt rested. And my sleep patterns were reversed, sleeping during the day and despairing in the night. When I should have been counting stars, I was picking at scars, the kind that form in the soul when pain is unaddressed.

Weight. Mine, at one point, dropped to eighty-five pounds. I mostly drank coffee and smoked cigarettes. Need I say more?

These are some of the most telling symptoms of depression. There are others, but here's the great news—no, let's raise the bar . . . here's the *good news*: because of the gospel of Christ we have the resources of heaven at our disposal. Add to that the counsel of his Word, which will assist us in building a life of emotional sanity. And Christ, who will companion us on our journey . . . all the way home. No more can kicking. That childish game is done. Instead we will become stargazers who acknowledge and applaud the Designer of us and them.

He counts the number of the stars; He
calls them all by name.—Psalm 147:4

If you need help, tell someone who has the ability to assist you.
If they don't, tell someone else. Be tenacious. You are worth it.

1. Why do you think God counted the stars and named them?
2. When did you go through a kick-the-can season?
3. How do you combat the enemy's propaganda?

TWENTY-FIVE
edit

He who has knowledge spares his words.

—PROVERBS 17:27

When Luci Swindoll told me one of her favorite inventions was the alphabet, I knew we would always be friends. I love words. I'm a bona fide verbiage collector. I love small words like *gnu*, descriptive words like *dollop*, and filler words like *thingamajigs* and *whatchamacallits*.

There's something magical about lining up letters and finding the very thing you want to say. So imagine the jolt I got when a couple of my friends showed up at a conference sporting "On

Voice Rest" badges. *What does that mean?* I puzzled. They rolled their eyes and pointed at the confusing script. "On voice rest," I squawked. Still befuddled, I asked, "Does that mean you're actually not going to talk?" They nodded. I was almost silenced, but then I rallied and decided I could talk for all three of us. I was chatting away when one of them got up, walked over to me, and pulled from her pocket a backup badge and pinned it on my collar. *Humph.*

C'mon, not talk? Think. About. It.

I read once about a movie actor who fasted from words on Wednesdays. He said it added a flurry of creative energy to his work and it helped him be more word sensitive and word selective when he did speak.

Secretly I admired his choice, but I have yet to duplicate it. I have, however, remained silent on two-hour flights only to get off and magpie anyone within a ten-foot perimeter. It's like the accrued word count within me percolated in my silence so that when I disembarked I erupted into a volley of caffeinated chat.

I do have a propensity to go on and on. I know that. It's like I have no Edit button. When in truth, I know it's a matter of changing gears (slowing my pace) and installing a conscious (Holy Spirit) awareness of my need to at least minimize my word count.

Voice rest has multiple benefits. Here are a few:

- Those who have grown weary of our deluge are relieved.
- We listen more closely because we are not busy crafting our response.
- Our new discipline will spill over into other frayed areas of our life.

- People's trust in us grows.
- Our center stills. We feel less frantic and, surprisingly, more heard.

So what about a wordless Wednesday or having a Mute button installed for Monday mornings? Or being silent long enough to hear what God's curriculum is for us?

> Silence is the sleep that nourishes
> wisdom.—Francis Bacon

Les and I find at this stage of our twirling, age-aching lives we must caution ourselves about our words lest we slip into a groundswell of grumbling. Nothing is worse than resorting to an organ recital in a group conversation. Really, who needs to hear about our innards besides our doctor? But I admit it's a temptation.

I have always been a talker. Yet over the years I have also learned to be a listener and to be quiet. But when I have a spell of words, watch out. I gust. High velocity. And once I gain momentum it's hard to tether my tongue. I have discovered the hard way the importance of learning to edit my output before I hurt someone's feelings or obligate myself beyond good judgment or exaggerate.

Here are two steps that will help if you, too, are given to gusts:

First, *practice silence at home*. Make friends with silent spaces. No television. No iTunes. Just you and the quiet. It's unnatural at first because we live in a noisy world, so we forget the soul-wash of silence. But when you adjust, you learn that quiet is a peacemaking friend who brings a sackful of sanity, and I guarantee you'll want to take it on the road with you.

Second, *practice asking questions.* When we are talking we are not learning. It helps if we ask questions instead of having all the answers. This will benefit us because first off we'll learn something; second, we will bless the person we ask because few people do; and lastly, it will provide us with an opportunity to put our self-editing skills into practice.

The first words of a woman that we are privy to in Scripture are in Eve's conversation with the serpent in the garden of Eden. Unfortunately, she takes time to converse with the enemy who has targeted her for destruction. In doing so, Eve is deceived, and in turn she uses her influence to draw her husband into their downfall.

The next thing we hear is Adam blaming Eve and Eve blaming the serpent, so the word games begin.

I know Eve must have had many conversations with Adam and with the Lord during the walks in the cool of the evening, but those are not recorded. The Genesis account goes from creation right to the fall. I would have loved to hear how the first lady spent her time in the beginning. And what she thought of the first daffodils, lilacs, and lavender. And did she ever sleep in a tree, sing with bluebirds, or ride on a zebra? What was her home like? Perhaps a tent of palm fronds encircled in orchids and lit by fireflies.

Evidently God thought it more important to cut to the chase. Eve got herself in trouble because she took time to have an exchange with Satan and then believed his words over God's. What a caution to us. We must remember that the enemy is cunning and will insinuate, placing words of doubt in our minds, to undermine our faith. His tactics haven't changed since the garden, and neither have our weaknesses. God has given us warning and weapons for warfare to protect us from the evil one.

For me, if I can keep tabs on the quality of my thought life, it improves my chances that my words will be quality as well. And quality serves me far better than quantity. My heart is hushed as I read verses from Proverbs . . .

- "Even a fool is counted wise when he holds his peace; when he shuts his lips, he is considered perceptive" (17:28).
- "Any fool can start a quarrel" (20:3).
- "Do you see a man hasty in his words? There is more hope for a fool than for him" (29:20).

That's clear. But admittedly not easy. It takes a constant effort to maintain a healthy thought life, one full of generosity and kindness toward ourselves and others. And while at first blush that sounds simple, think about the last person who hurt your feelings. Were your thoughts pleasant, merciful, and full of forgiveness? How about your words? It takes a current ongoing conversation with Jesus to remind me of my options, because my tendency is to be retaliatory, moody, and gossipy. All which lead to a sick soul life, an uneasy thought life, and verbiage that reeks of hostility. Instead, I'm called to be forgiving, sweet, and constrained. This is definitely going to take a work of God.

Inside words are the kindling for outside words, which is why our inside conversations need to be examined. Here are a few things that help with my inside talk:

- *Scripture*. It reminds me in a thousand ways that "death and life are in the power of the tongue" (Proverbs 18:21).
- *Meditation*. Thinking on things that are good and true lead to good and true exchanges with others. I like to sit under the tutelage of a Bible verse, asking the Holy Spirit to lead and guide me into the truth of it.
- *People*. It helps to have strong examples speaking life-giving words around us. They help keep us on track.
- *Books*. Study worthwhile material that stirs up a healthy resolve within you. I read everything from Chuck Swindoll to Shakespeare and Moore to Malachi. I keep stacks of books around my house for easy access to inspire me and my guests. Also wholesome magazines, life-grabbing quotes, and heart-revealing poetry.

I find it helpful to pray before I unleash myself on the public. That helps me to set my mind in a self-editing direction. Especially on those days when I'm moody, cranky, sanguine, or sensitive, which happens basically on weekdays and weekends.

Dear Lord, you had James warn us how unruly our words can be, so we are aware of our need for your intervention on our behalf. You have given us the power to uplift others as we speak words of life. May we be wise enough to relinquish our right to be right and instead be loving while retaining honesty and kindness. May our words and our motives meet with your holy inspection. Amen.

1. Do you have too many words? Or too few?
2. Where is your guarded space for quiet?
3. Who are your examples? What is their style of truth telling?

TWENTY-SIX
story

Fill your paper with the breathings of your heart.

—WILLIAM WORDSWORTH

Ever think you'd like to write your story? Me too. But I didn't imagine it would happen. Dreams can come true . . . but it may be a circuitous route. One full of windows, wind shears, and wonder.

I encourage you to write, because no one knows your journey better than you. Besides, would you want your relatives to write about your life from their view? I rest my case. You are the only one who knows how you felt and why you did some of the things you did, and you are the only one who has access to your secrets. Even if your story never makes it into mainstream publishing, penning it can be healing and offer documentation for yourself and your family . . . for generations.

I giggled at Churchill's statement:

> History will be kind to me, for I intend
> to write it.—Sir Winston Churchill

In the writing of your journey be prepared for the Lord to teach you about yourself, your family, and his hand upon you long before you realized it. Looking back can strengthen your ability to look forward. It's important to own your history because God gave us invaluable information in our yesterdays that offer us a greater education than any degree we could earn. Yesterday is what compassions today and mercies tomorrow.

I'm not saying live in yesterday. I'm not saying get stuck in an old drama. I'm not saying rehearse or rehash pain. But you may have to hold it for a moment; that's what makes us more human and tender. My advice would be to visit yesterday as you would an old aunt: take a fistful of violets and tea for her, not a nightgown and toothbrush for you.

Your story could one day be a book. And I know even the sound of writing a book can be intimidating. Questions immediately taunt us. *Where do I start? How do I know when I'm done? How long should it take?* These questions alone can cause one to hesitate.

Today having a book has never been easier. You can write it, upload it, and *bam!* It's a done deal. Well, not exactly. The writing part alone can be a sticky wicket. I have an ongoing battle whenever I start a manuscript. Here's my scenario: I sit down to write, and up comes a pressing need to clean out my closets and drawers. The thought pulsates inside me until it overtakes my brain and I make a wild dash to my closet. No kidding. Every. Single. Time. This cleaning frenzy never occurs otherwise. No sudden impulses arise to sort and tidy or purge and pitch until its book-writing time. I believe this condition has a name: Mrs. Sabotage. And her husband, Mr. Procrastination. And their twins, Excuses and Blame.

Then there's the "I need to go to the beach to be inspired" excuse about writing. Or "I need to check into a spa" aria. Or "if I had a week in Paris" dream. Truth is, often the more beautiful our surroundings, the more distracting they can be. I mean, who wants to be staring at a screen squeezing out letters when one could be eating warm French rolls with slices of pâté and fragrant Brie, slathered in fresh peaches? See what I mean? Yes, sights and smells are a lovely distraction, but a book they do not make. If you are oblivious to delicious surroundings and not tempted to eat your weight in croissants, then absolutely pack your iPad and head for Paris. (Take me, please. I'll wait for you at the bakery.)

Instead, I suggest you get hammer and nails and affix your britches to a chair. I write in airplanes, airports, my living room, my office, hotel rooms, coffee shops where other writers are pounding the keys, on the porch, in bed (I know, I know, but I do), and in long lines. I didn't purpose to write all over God's green earth, but between my speaking and travel I had to do it that way, or not at all. And I really wanted to write and was committed to meet my deadlines. In being forced to write anywhere, I learned it was possible. I wouldn't have believed it otherwise, at least not of myself.

I held a romantic view of writers and their work until I became one. Writing is a glorious, gutsy grind. I had no idea of the difficulty factor or frustration. So why am I encouraging you to do it? Because misery loves company? Actually, and might I say, gratefully, mixed in the challenge is the joy of the creative process and then the sweet victory of completion.

So don't give up because your brain feels like a clump of clover; don't wait to start your writing until you have the "time" or until you feel inspired. Don't hold your breath for tingly feelings to fill your fingertips before you start typing or penning or recording. I have found inspiration usually percolates in the midst of sweat and tears, and often is not recognized for its genius until later.

Here are a few tips that help me on a writing project:

Do your homework. Visit a bookstore and see how others have approached their stories. Allow those who have gone before you to mentor you. What captures your interest? And why? Look at what is on the best-seller list to gain a sense of what the public is drawn to as far as titles, designs, and topics. Sometimes it teaches you what you want to do and sometimes what you'll never do. Although "never" is a long time.

Have a loose plan for your project, one that allows you to adjust as the book forms. Your writing may decide to take you down paths you hadn't imagined. Those paths will either be divine leadings or rabbit twirls, I mean, trails. Rabbit trails are usually a form of sabotage or signs of an undisciplined mind (one of my hurdles), whereas divine leadings are revelations for you the writer and then to bless your reader. Divine leadings cheer on our hearts as writers, so we don't give up. It's the line that marries well, the paragraph that sings, and the chapter that harmonizes with itself and the book's best intentions.

When I say we need to have a loose plan, we do also need some semblance of order. A clear outline for your work is of foundational, organizational, and directional benefit. For instance, to write your life story you might divide it into years, or houses you've lived in, or a division as simple as yesterday, today, and tomorrow. You might want to separate your life into your first family, education, career, and marriage (if applicable). Or if your story is one of travel, you could break it up into places you've visited and sights you've seen. If you are an artist you might want to use the names of colors to paint your story into the minds of readers. I divided my biography by people: my mom, dad, brother, sister, grandma, husband, friends—telling how they impacted my life.

When possible have a provocative opening line(s). One that catches people's attention and represents your life (subject matter). For instance, I might say: "In 1945, the war ended and my life began." Or, "On my knees digging up potatoes in the noon sun to earn money for cigarettes, it struck me that being a runaway was no fun. No fun at all."

Try it. Think about your life, isolate an event, and reduce it to a sentence that could entice a reader to want more.

Let your work "air out." Step away from your efforts from time to time so when you come back to it, you can see it with fresh eyes. Read your work out loud. Sometimes your ear will catch what your eye misses. If a sentence is laborious to read out loud, it will be sluggish for a reader to understand. Sacrifice it, and try saying it another, more succinct way.

Don't fall too in love with flowery descriptions. You may have to weed-whack a few blossoms for the good of the garden. Don't get stuck thinking there's only one effective way to say something. Trust me, there are hundreds of fragrant approaches that will work as well . . . if not better. (Writing is humbling work.)

Edit with a vengeance. Better to say a little well than to spew endlessly. A life reminder for me (whether speaking or writing) has been, "The key to longevity is brevity." I tend to be a pendulum swinging from being too word thrifty and leaving too many unanswered questions, to being downright verbose. Neither extreme produces a healthy manuscript.

This is where an editor is invaluable. If you plan on publishing your manuscript, submit it willingly into the hands of an experienced editor. Warning: don't take the edits personally. We need to see it as part of our ongoing education. We need their expertise and objectivity. Did I mention writing is humbling? (I admit it is possible to get an ill fit with an editor who rakes your work over the coals of their personal disillusionment. You don't want someone who sacrifices your style to impose their own. That's not acceptable.)

Most of the time an editor's contributions are not directed against us but toward the rules of writing and the goal of wholeness and continuity. I was blessed for many years with the expertise of an editor who made me a better writer (and person) than I would have been without her. Most editors deserve badges of valor and paid vacations.

A tendency of new writers is to overpunctuate. Overpunctuating is like twirling too fast: it discombobulates the reader. Go easy. Especially with exclamation points and commas. When I wrote my first book more than twenty years ago, my opening chapter looked like it had the exclamation measles (until my editor cured it and me). Besides, if we need a boatload of punctuations to add emphasis, we should reweigh our word choices and add stronger, livelier words. Ones with their own nerve and verve that can stand and shout without the need of a prop to hold them up.

> The difference between the right word and the almost right word is the difference between lightning and a lightning bug.—Mark Twain

Did I confess I love writing . . . when I'm not dreading it? It is my dearest friend and my worst enemy. It taunts me, teases me, and transforms me. One minute I'm under its intoxicating spell, and the next I'm saying words about it that my mom cautioned me were rude.

Often my writing reveals things to me about myself I didn't know. Sometimes that's heartening and sometimes dismantling. I have found that the more I risk being vulnerable in my work, the more I strengthen in my weak places. And the more my readers respond. (But privacy boundaries are also imperative.)

> No tears in the writer, no tears in the reader. No surprise in the writer, no surprise in the reader.—Robert Frost

Without written language where would we be? No books? What a dreadful thought. I need your story. Life is lonely. And hard. And incredibly good. Your story reminds me I'm not alone or as odd as I thought. Company breeds community. Let's pen our way into each other's presence.

May Christ be our guiding light.

1. If you wrote your story, what would you title it?
2. If your story was a movie, who would you like to play the part of you?
3. When did you last read a biography? Who was it about?
4. Who is your favorite author?
5. What do you like about that author's work?

conclusion

As a dancer shifts his position he keeps his balance. He does this by taking his center with him. He shifts his center of gravity, re-establishing equilibrium in the very instant he has leapt.

—MARY CAROLINE RICHARD, *Centering
in Pottery, Poetry and the Person*

Christ came that we might experience abundant life and joy overflowing. So how do we get there from here? I don't have a full map, but I have picked up a few road signs on my journey that may be of help.

Knowing is the first step toward grasping a truth, while owning it in our inward parts is another huge leap. My knower knows far more than I live, which is true for most of us. Fully owning truth is a slow process and a grow process. One that is secured by asking the Lord to help us incorporate the changes we need to be fully alive.

Let's talk about integration, the act of allowing the things in this book that rang true for you to be personally owned. For years I thought studying God's Word was enough. I thought if it's in my head, it's in my heart. But memorizing, as helpful a discipline as that is, is not internalizing. Head knowledge and heart knowledge live acres apart down a winding road. With speed bumps . . . so pack a lunch.

Have more questions than answers. Having questions shows humility, interest in others, and a teachable spirit—all qualities that please the Lord and help with our own integration "therapy." Wait for people to ask before offering your insight. It will improve their attention, deepen their appreciation, and teach us discipline. When we think we know what's right for others, it casts shadows on our own path. While we are called to be available and supportive of others, we don't actually know what God is up to inside them. God is under no obligation to explain himself (even though I'd appreciate it if he would). And just because God worked one way in my circumstances doesn't mean that's his plan for someone else. So proceed carefully in finalizing God's intentions and the execution of his will in regard to someone else's life.

Also, when we ask questions, we put ourselves in the position of a student. There's no telling what God will reveal to us, often from a most unlikely source. God loves to use the unlikely to perform the impossible, to demonstrate the outrageousness of his love.

Pay attention. My husband always says he's too broke to pay attention. The truth is its costly not to pay the price attention requires; otherwise, if we don't learn along the way our closing life chapter will be entitled "Bankrupt." The dailyness of life affords us tons of insight meant to help us make wise choices. So take notes on life and people. Even bad examples are teeming with good counsel.

Recently I watched a woman scream her head off in an airport because something didn't go her way. And I do mean scream. She gathered quite a crowd. Haven't you witnessed radical public behavior? Like someone is trying out for a sci-fi movie?

But I've also seen people who handled their inconveniences and disruptions with the strength of grace, maintaining their dignity while making their point. They are the ones who sleep well at night, make sterling a standard, and mercy others.

That ranting screamer plays in my head like a viral video clip when I am tempted to go hormonal on someone. Then I think, *I don't want to be that person. She was rude, offensive, and I felt embarrassed for her. I have options.* I choose to pull instead from the mental notes I made of the person whose grace made space for her.

That is not to say I haven't been the rude, disruptive one. I remember only too well my uncalled-for behavior several years ago in Jerusalem with a cab driver who was overcharging us. I was, how shall I say, unattractive in my behavior. Like a sci-fi character. And to think I was in Jerusalem, where Jesus walked. I would gladly pay the cabbie a double fee today if I could take back my reaction.

Gratefully, I also remember an encounter with a visitor in an art store while in Jerusalem, where our conversation was attended by angels. It truly felt like a divine appointment. The presence of Christ was so palpable that my friends rushed to me when we got outside and asked what holy thing had transpired.

To think I was both the sci-fi contestant and the servant offering Christ's love to a dying man. What a cracked pot.

We are all fractured and in need of God's mercy and mending. Some are just more obvious, like me and the screecher. Jesus has promised to be our Wonderful Counselor, so we'd be wise to take him up on his offer. If you feel a tug on your heart while reading a chapter in this book or answering a question, I recommend stopping and camping out there. Pitch a tent, light a fire, and ask the Lord what he wants you to learn or know more deeply before you move on. Don't miss it. Journal what you're hearing. Christ is all about revelation, and he longs to show us in personal ways how to live a more honorable life full of compassion and content.

Twirl is a term we usually reserve for children—and gratefully, we are. We are the Lord's children, and while he instructs us to put away childish things, he implores us to come to him like a child: wide-eyed with wonder, trust, and a rejoicing heart.

Wonder, trust, and a rejoicing heart. That, my friend, is how one gets her twirl on and discovers a fresh spin on life!

> *Growing up*
> *I was not allowed*
> *to dance.*
>
> *I was given a long list of reasons why,*
> *none of which belong in a poem.*
>
> *But I've seen babies dance*
> *and birds pirouette*
> *and horses prance*
> *I've seen sailboats waltz with the ocean*
> *Why, even runaway plastic bags*
> *leap and twirl in the wind!*
>
> *When the spirit dances,*
> *will the body follow?*

STEPHANIE EDDLEMAN

Chapter 5

1. Craig Freudenrich, Ph.D. and Robynne Boyd, "How Your Brain Works," How Stuff Works, http://science.howstuffworks.com /life/inside-the-mind/human-brian/brain1.htm.
2. "About the Library: General Information," Library of Congress, http://www.loc.gov/about/generalinfo.html.
3. Lewis Smede, *How Can It Be All Right When Everything Is All Wrong?* (Colorado Springs: Shaw, 2000).

Chapter 7

1. *Wikipedia*, s.v. "Columbidae," last modified May 30, 2013, http://en .wikipedia.org/wiki/Columbidae.

Chapter 8

1. Pamela Gerloff, "Are You Meeting Your Laugh Quota? Why You Should Laugh Like a 5-Year-Old," *Psychology Today,* June 21, 2011, http://www.psychologytoday.com/blog/the-possibility -paradigm/201106/are-you-meeting-your-laugh-quota-why-you -should-laugh-5-year-ol.

Chapter 9

1. Evelyn Christenson, *Lord, Change Me* (Colorado Springs: Cook, 2002).

Chapter 10

1. "Interesting Facts About Pens and Pencils," PenFactory.com, November 29, 2011, http://blog.penfactory.com/?p=82.

Chapter 14

1. Joe Verghese et al., "Leisure Activities and the Risk of Dementia in the Elderly," *New England Journal of Medicine*, June 19, 2003, 348: 2508–16, http://www.nejm.org/doi/full/10.1056/NEJMoa 022252.

2. http://www.nia.nih.gov/.

Chapter 15

1. "Most Expensive Perfume Bottles in the World," World Most Expensive, April 18, 2013, http://world-most-expensive.info /most-expensive-perfume-bottles-in-the-world/.

Chapter 22

1. "U.S. Pet Ownership Statistics," The Humane Society of the United States, August 12, 2011, http://www.humanesociety.org /issues/pet_overpopulation/facts/pet_ownership_statistics.html.

acknowledgments

I guarantee that no one writes a book alone. Oh, we may pen the words, but many others have been our teachers, examples, and the ones who research a quote, or fine-tune a paragraph, or design a cover. Also, there are those valiant ones who protect our time and space so we can press our thoughts on a page.

I twirl with gratitude that God has brought so many exceptional people into my life. So here's my shout-out list full of thank-you's and hallelujahs:

Danya Clairmont, my own personal Wonder Woman who keeps my office running and who makes me appear smarter than I am. She understands my quirkiness and my hopscotch way of thinking and interprets me to others. Thank you dear daughter-in-law.

Mike Atkins, for all you do to keep my speaking and writing world from turning topsy-turvy, I'm grateful. Big thanks to Katie Williams for valuable research and for always being a joy. Nita Andrews, the Lord knew how I'd need your prayers and inspiration. You make me think wide Technicolor thoughts. Karen Anderson, big hugs to you for your last-minute creative nudges—they were truly encouraging.

To the folks at Thomas Nelson, thank you for filling the world with truth. Adria Haley, Julie Allen, Mallory Perkins, Jennifer Stair, Jenna Schrader, and Anna Floit, thanks for making *Twirl* so spiffy. I'm delighted to call publisher Matt Baugher coworker and friend. Thank you for including me in your writer lineup.

about the author

An original Women of Faith speaker, Patsy Clairmont's quick wit and depth of biblical knowledge combine in a powerful pint-size package. A former agoraphobe with a pronounced funny bone, Patsy speaks to women from all walks of life.

Patsy is a bookish woman who loves words and has a penchant for dark chocolate sorbet. Since spelling bees in grade school, childhood Scrabble games, right up to her current addiction with Words with Friends, she has been known to spell it out, to say it like it is.

Patsy never imagined the expansive plans God had in mind for her. She just wanted to make it to her neighborhood grocery store and safely home again. Instead, for the past thirty-five years she has been traipsing throughout the U.S. and Canada, and has spoken to millions of women (and men) offering spiritual and emotional hope.

Patsy's current passion is helping people shake loose the stories from their own lives to use in communicating more personally, effectively, and memorably, whether from a stage or over the back fence with a neighbor. Pasty and her husband, Les, live in Tennessee.

www.patsyclairmont.com